W9-BUE-018

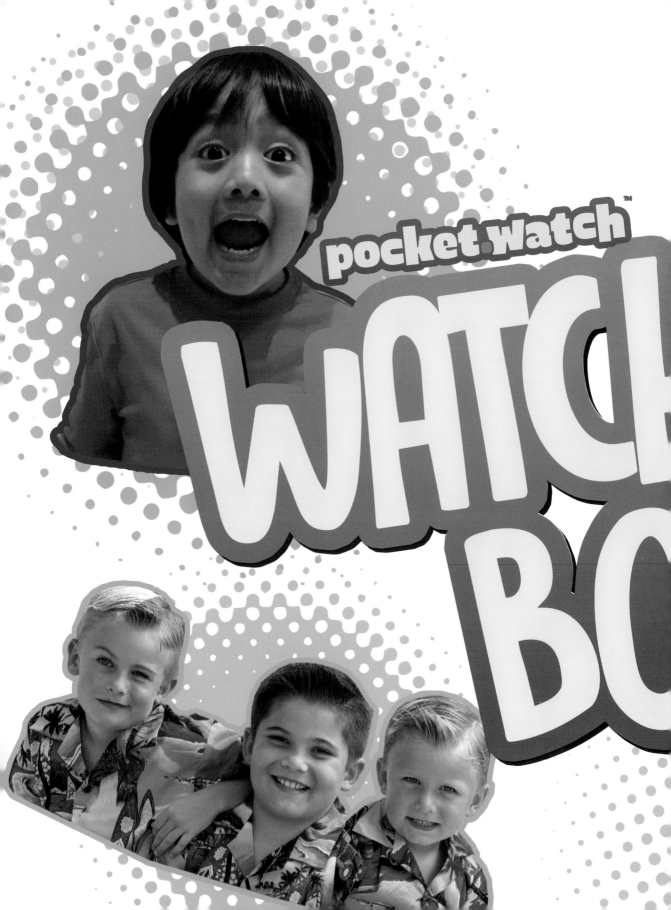

pocket.watch ™

WATCH
BO

Inside the World of YouTube Stars

Ryan ToysReview, HobbyKidsTV, JillianTubeHD, and EvanTubeHD

ʰ THIS

OK!

Simon Spotlight
New York London Toronto Sydney New Delhi

SIMON SPOTLIGHT
An imprint of Simon & Schuster Children's Publishing Division
1230 Avenue of the Americas, New York, New York 10020
This Simon Spotlight edition October 2018
Text by Aubre Andrus
© 2018 PocketWatch, Inc. The pocket.watch logo is a trademark of PocketWatch, Inc. All Rights Reserved.
Ryan ToysReview: Ryan ToysReview is a registered trademark of RTR Production, LLC, RFR Entertainment, Inc. and
Remka, Inc. All Rights Reserved. All intellectual property and names associated with Ryan ToysReview are trademarks or
registered trademarks of RTR Production, LLC, RFR Entertainment, Inc. and Remka, Inc. All Rights Reserved.
HobbyKidsTV: HobbyKidsTV is a registered trademark of Mini Flix Media, Inc. All Rights Reserved. All intellectual property
and names associated with HobbyKidsTV are trademarks or registered trademarks of Mini Flix Media, Inc.
All Rights Reserved.
EvanTubeHD and JillianTubeHD: EvanTubeHD and JillianTubeHD are trademarks of Power Pixel Entertainment, Inc.
All Rights Reserved. All intellectual property and names associated with EvanTubeHD and JillianTubeHD are trademarks
or registered trademarks of Power Pixel Entertainment, Inc. All Rights Reserved.
CaptainSparklez: Captain Sparklez is a registered trademark of Jordan Maron, Incorporated. All Rights Reserved. All
intellectual property and names associated with Captain Sparklez are trademarks or registered trademarks of Jordan
Maron, Incorporated. All Rights Reserved.
Stock photos copyright © 2018 istock.com
All other photos:
pocket.watch: © 2018 PocketWatch, Inc. All Rights Reserved.
Ryan ToysReview: © 2018 RTR Production, LLC, RFR Entertainment, Inc. and Remka, Inc.
All Rights Reserved.
HobbyKidsTV: © 2018 Mini Flix Media, Inc. All Rights Reserved.
EvanTubeHD and JillianTubeHD: © 2018 Power Pixel Entertainment, Inc. All Rights Reserved.
CaptainSparklez: © 2018 Jordan Maron, Incorporated. All Rights Reserved.
All rights reserved, including the right of reproduction in whole or in part in any form.
SIMON SPOTLIGHT and colophon are registered trademarks of Simon & Schuster, Inc.
For more information about special discounts for bulk purchases, please contact
Simon & Schuster Special Sales at 1-866-506-1949 or business@simonandschuster.com.
Manufactured in the United States of America 0918 LAK
10 9 8 7 6 5 4 3 2 1
ISBN 978-1-5344-2870-6
ISBN 978-1-5344-2871-3 (eBook)

Contents

Hi from CaptainSparklez!

Hi! CaptainSparklez here. I am super excited to welcome you to *Watch This Book!* You might know me from my online videos. I post about everything from gaming to music and anything else that interests me. I've been making videos for more than eight years, and I'm loving it.

I'm also a part of the **pocket.watch** family, just like the seriously awesome stars of this book:

Spend the day with Ryan from **Ryan ToysReview**. Ryan checks out the latest toys, does supercool science experiments, and plays video games . . . like me!

You'll also hang out with the Hobbykids from **HobbyKidsTV**. You probably know these three brothers from their GIANT surprise eggs.

Then go visit Jillian from **JillianTubeHD**. She posts creative craft videos and vlogs. She's a great singer, too. And get to know her brother, Evan, from **EvanTubeHD**. His challenge videos are totally hilarious! There's never a dull moment in Evan and Jillian's house!

Watch this book and enter the world of these YouTube stars. You'll meet their families, learn fun facts, and even play games together. When you finish this book, you'll be the ultimate expert on Ryan, the Hobbykids, Jillian, and Evan!

So what are you waiting for?

WATCH IT.
READ IT.
LOVE IT!

Hi! I'm Ryan!

You might know me from my YouTube channel Ryan ToysReview. I review toys like LEGOs, monster trucks, and more. I also like to test out science experiments and play video games. My mommy, daddy, and twin sisters star in my videos too.

If I had to pick one word to describe myself, it would be **"curious."** I always ask a lot of questions. My parents say that I'm very outgoing and sociable and that I'm a caring brother to my little sisters.

Age: 7
Height: 43 inches
(3½ feet)
Hair color:
Dark brown
Eye color:
Dark brown

My Favorite . . .

Ice cream flavor: vanilla

Foods: pizza and oranges

Subjects: math and music

Sports: soccer and tennis

Animals: panda and dinosaur

Books: Little Critter series

Holiday: Christmas

Season: summer

Colors: neon green and neon blue

Drink: milk

Number: infinity

Emoji: 🙂

Playground activity: running around

Superhero: Batman

Watch Me!

How I Got Started

When I was three years old, I loved watching other people on YouTube. One day I asked my mommy if we could have our own channel. She said **yes**! We did it just for fun. My first video was about a LEGO train. I liked making the video, so we kept making more. We never ran out of ideas of what to film. We just made videos about things I liked.

Since then, my parents, my sisters, and I have uploaded about **one thousand** videos! Now they're about more than just toys. We do skits, challenges, animation, science experiments, gaming, and more. The videos are still just as fun to make.

Q: When do you make your videos?

A: We usually film over the weekend during my sisters' naptimes. Each episode usually takes thirty minutes to film.

What It's Really Like to Be on YouTube

It's really exciting to be on YouTube. I love when kids tell me they like my videos. When I got one million subscribers, YouTube gave me a trophy called the Gold Play Button. Because I have more than ten million subscribers now, I will get a Diamond Play Button award soon.

In every video, we make sure to say good-bye and thank our fans for watching–and we always make sure that we're all having fun playing together. We laugh a lot in our videos.

Q: What's your favorite part about being on YouTube?

A: I love going on pretend play adventures.

Q: What's your least favorite part about being on YouTube?

A: Cleaning up.

Inside Ryan ToysReview

SUBSCRIBERS: 15.3 million+

UPLOADING SINCE: March 2015

TOTAL VIEWS: 23.4 billion+

OTHER CHANNELS: Ryan's Family Review, VTubers, Combo Panda, Gus the Gummy Gator, the Studio Space

My Most-Watched Video

We got more than one billion views on a "Huge Eggs Surprise Toys Challenge" video. I had to climb around a huge inflatable water slide and collect giant colorful eggs. The slide was much bigger than me—even taller than my parents! We set it up in our backyard. It looked like a playground. It had a climbing wall, a fort, and a long slide with a sprinkler that ended in a pool of water. The eggs were hidden everywhere! Once I collected them all, I was finally allowed to crack them open. There were toy cars and action figures inside.

Q: What do you do if a video doesn't work out the way you expected?

A: If it's still fun to watch, we call it an epic fail video. Maybe other people can learn from our mistakes!

My Longest Video to Film

The longest time it ever took to film a video was an hour and a half, because we were trying to make a giant chocolate egg and it kept cracking! When you make chocolate eggs, you have to let them harden in a mold. But then removing them from the mold can be really tricky! It's easy for them to break.

Q: What do you think about millions of people watching you?

A: That's a lot of people!

Q: What inspires you?

A: Watching other kids have fun, and having fun with my family.

17

Sometimes We Get Messy!

Once we filled our bathroom with Orbeez.

Orbeez are tiny beads that grow bigger when they are placed in water. They look like marbles but they are squishy.

The floor was covered in Orbeez. My toy trains kept slipping and falling over. Then I buried the trains in a bathtub full of Orbeez. I had a lot of fun playing, but it took forever to clean up. It felt like there were a million beads everywhere!

Try It Yourself: The Orbeez Challenge

Another way to play with Orbeez is to do the Orbeez Challenge! Have someone hide small toys in a container full of Orbeez. You can use marbles or cotton balls too. No peeking! Then race a friend or sibling to see who can find the most toys in the shortest amount of time.

My Messiest Video Ever!

It's actually a video that we never got to post! We tried the Exploding Watermelon Challenge. We took a break from putting rubber bands around the watermelon and decided to finish the video the next day. We brought the watermelon inside and put it in the laundry room. I didn't see it happen, but it exploded during the night. It was a mess! We didn't get to film the explosion. I had to help my daddy clean it up.

The Exploding Watermelon Challenge

See how many rubber bands you can slip around a watermelon before it explodes. You'll need a lot of large rubber bands. The pressure eventually causes the watermelon to literally explode. Make sure you do this challenge outside, because it can get really messy!

⚠ DON'T TRY THIS YOURSELF. ALWAYS DO THIS CHALLENGE WITH AN ADULT. AND ALWAYS WEAR SAFETY GOGGLES.

I Love My Fans!

A lot of people watch my YouTube videos. That means people might recognize me when I leave the house—people I don't even know yet!

I don't mind, though. My fans are always super nice and friendly when I see them in real life. They usually want to tell me that they watch my videos on YouTube. They feel like I'm already their friend! It's cool.

Kids feel like they know me when they meet me. We always have a lot in common. But I bet you have a lot in common with other kids too!

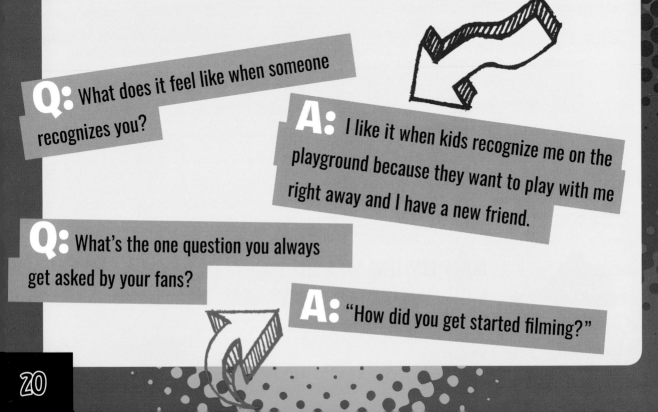

Q: What does it feel like when someone recognizes you?

A: I like it when kids recognize me on the playground because they want to play with me right away and I have a new friend.

Q: What's the one question you always get asked by your fans?

A: "How did you get started filming?"

How to Make a New Friend

According to Ryan!

1. Say hi!
Don't be shy. Just walk up and say hi to a kid on the playground or at school.

2. Introduce yourself.
Tell them your name and how old you are. Ask them what their name is.

3. Invite them to play with you.
Ask if they'd like to play a game with you or join you on the playground.

4. Ask what they like.
You might find that you have a favorite toy, TV show, or video game in common.

Q: What's the craziest thing you've ever been asked by a fan?

A: "How are you here? I saw you on my iPad!"

SEE, IT'S EASY AND FUN TO MAKE A NEW FRIEND!

A Day in My Life

Good morning!

On weekdays, my mommy wakes me up for school. I brush my teeth and brush my hair. Sometimes I just make my hair messier, so Mommy helps me.

Then I change into my clothes. Decisions, decisions!

Yum!

I eat breakfast in the kitchen—usually cereal with milk.

23

My sisters!

Then I say good morning to my **sisters**. I have twin sisters named **Emma** and **Kate**. Some people think they look the same, but I can always tell them apart. Their birthday is in the summer and they just turned two years old. I play with them all the time. We love to play chase and hide-and-seek.

If I had to use one word to describe my twin sisters, it would be "**energetic**." They really like watching and dancing to nursery rhyme videos.

My Sisters' Favorite . . .

Food: chopped grapes

Playground activities: slide and playing chase

Drink: milk . . . just like me!

Ice cream flavor: vanilla . . . just like me!

Hobbies: playing and drawing

Animal: cat

Mommy!

Daddy!

I also say GOOD MORNING to my **mommy** and **daddy**. Before we made YouTube videos together, my mommy was a high school chemistry teacher and my daddy was a structural engineer. Chemistry is a type of science where people study the matter that makes up our world. A structural engineer helps to build things like buildings and bridges. Cool, right?

I'm very shy in front of the camera, but Ryan always helps me act funny in the videos.

I've had no acting experience whatsoever. But I'm not nervous. I'm just filming at home so I'm in my natural setting. I just have fun!

HEY, PARENTS!

Want to make YouTube videos with your kids? Ryan's mom and dad have advice.

🔊 **Do what the kids enjoy.**

We started making LEGO and Thomas & Friends videos because that's what Ryan liked. Now we still play with some toys, but we do more skits and gaming videos. We try to evolve the channel with Ryan's interests.

🔊 **Start with a low budget.**

Film with your phone, cheap lights, and a cheap background. Grow the budget as you grow the channel.

🔊 **Be authentic.**

It's all about the connection. A lot of kids tell us that when they watch Ryan's videos, they feel like they are watching their friend.

Q&A WITH RYAN'S MOM AND DAD!

Q: What do you want to be doing five years from now?

A: Making fun animation for kids.

Q: What do you like to watch on YouTube (besides your own channel)?

A: News and educational videos about humans and animals.

Next I put on my shoes and grab my backpack. My mommy drives me to **school**.

The best part of the school day is math class.

I usually buy my **lunch**. I like eating ice cream sandwiches, milk, Goldfish, ketchup sandwiches, and string cheese.

After lunch I have **science class**. We learn about how volcanoes erupt.

A **volcano** is a hill or a mountain on the earth's crust that's connected to a magma chamber underground.

Magma is the name for liquid rock before it reaches the earth's surface. Once it reaches the surface, it's called lava!

Volcanoes erupt because of pressure in the earth's surface. Sometimes there is too much pressure and it just **explodes**!

It's like when you shake a soda can—the pressure builds until you open it. Then it releases with a ton of fizzy bubbles! The pressure pushes the magma up from underground and then it spills onto the earth's surface—now it's lava! Lava is a hot liquid that will harden once it's cooled.

Active volcanoes could erupt at any moment. Dormant volcanoes haven't erupted for more than two hundred years, but they still could erupt in the future. Extinct volcanoes will never erupt again. There are scientists who study volcanoes so we know if they are about to erupt.

Did you know that the Hawaiian Islands were made from volcanoes?

Hawaii

I do a lot of science experiments on my channel too. My favorite was the Mentos and Diet Coke experiment. **SPOILER ALERT:** It explodes like an awesome rocket volcano show!

Mentos and Diet Coke Experiment

You will need:

> 2-liter bottle of Diet Coke
>
> Mentos candy

Take the bottle of Diet Coke and set it outside on a place that's okay to get messy, like a driveway or the grass in your backyard.

Remove the cap on the Diet Coke bottle, then drop one Mentos inside. Now run! A reaction will start immediately and spray into the air like a volcano.

⚠ DON'T TRY THIS YOURSELF. ALWAYS DO THIS CHALLENGE WITH AN ADULT.

In my video, we tried duct-taping a Diet Coke bottle to my toy dump truck to see if the reaction would make the truck move forward. It worked a little bit. Then we tried to attach two smaller Diet Coke bottles to the sides of my race cars to see if they would move. That was an EPIC FAIL!

One time we tried the experiment with my little sisters. **Emma** and **Kate** had never tried this before! We used small, medium, large, and extra-large bottles of soda. We set them in a plastic pool inside our house. One Mentos was enough to make the small soda fizz. In the medium soda, we put in two Mentos. That was a little bit bigger of an explosion, so my sisters were curious. We put three Mentos in the large and then four Mentos in the extra-large. Now we had a big explosion that really got my sisters' attention! **It made a mess**.

Next we tried putting five Mentos in diet soda versus regular soda. They both exploded the same. So then we tried twelve Mentos! We went outside for this experiment because we guessed that it would be messy. We were right! It made a **big explosion** and my sisters thought it was pretty cool. They're still really little so they can't say much, but I could tell they were excited.

Why Does This Happen?

When the candy drops into the soda, a lot of carbon dioxide gas is released. Carbon dioxide is what makes sodas bubbly. The more carbon dioxide, the more bubbles come out of the bottle!

1:30 p.m. Recess!

At school, sometimes we get extra recess. Awesome! My friends and I play a game of **Cool or Drool**. Play it with me! After each item, just tell me if you think it's "cool," which means you like it, or "drool," which means you're not that into it.

HERE ARE MY ANSWERS!

Rainbows ·· cool

Video games ·································· cool

Hedgehogs ····································· cool

Unicorns ······································· cool

Balloons ······································· cool

Snow ··· cool

The beach ····································· cool

Candy corn ··································· cool

Knock-knock jokes ························· cool

Pirates ································· cool

Scary stories ··························· drool

Slime ··································· cool

Boogers ·································· drool

Stickers ································· cool

Sleepovers ······························ cool

Pizza ·································· cool

Bugs ································· cool

Dinosaurs ······························ cool

Baths ·································· cool

Today we also have geography class. There are so many different places in the world! Some of my **FAVORITE** places are . . .

Disney World

The first ride I rode at Disney World was Splash Mountain, which is a log ride that ends in a big drop with a big splash. When we were waiting in line, a sign said, **YOU MAY GET WET.** We weren't even wearing pool clothes! But Mommy and I decided to try it anyway.

Once we got into the log, we climbed so high. I knew we were going to get so wet! At first there was just a little drop. We didn't get wet at all. But then we kept going. We were almost there! It was finally time for the big drop—*whoosh!* We got wet! It was really fun. I wasn't even scared.

The next time we rode Splash Mountain was at Disneyland. Mommy made me hold her hand as we went down the big drop! It was a ton of fun again.

Legoland

Legoland is a theme park filled with LEGOs! Building LEGOs is one of my favorite things ever. One of my favorite parts of Legoland is the hotel! It's filled with LEGOs. They even have **floating LEGOs** in the pool. You can build things that float!

We stayed in an Adventure-themed room with a LEGO monkey, spider, and scorpion. There were also tons of LEGOs to play with in our room, and a scavenger hunt. Besides a big bed for Mommy and Daddy, there were two bunk beds that I got to choose from. Five beds for only three people!

The restaurant had LEGO builds that looked good enough to eat. I wanted to eat the ice cream made from LEGOs, but instead I got myself some real ice cream. Mommy told me I had to eat dinner first, though.

Japan

Daddy surprised Mommy and me with a trip to Japan! There are a lot of fun places for kids there, like Universal Studios Japan and a train museum called the Railway Museum. They also have really, really fast trains. They go so fast, they are called bullet trains. In Japanese, they're called *shinkansen*. **I love trains!**

After school, I go to **music class**. We play songs and there are lots of instruments we can try, like the **drums**, **guitar**, **keyboard**, **shakers**, and more. Playing the guitar is fun. I also like playing the drums.

In music class, sometimes the guitar and piano have colors on them, which makes them easier to play. I like music a lot. Fast music is my favorite.

Song videos are one of my favorite kinds of YouTube videos to make. The body parts video was a fun one! It teaches kids the names of the body parts. My sisters like it too. They're in the video clapping. They look so cute. It's hard not to dance when you hear the song.

5:00 p.m. I'm Home!

After music class, I go home and do some **chores**. I don't get an allowance, but I help clean up the house once a week.

I **wipe up** the dining room table and living room table with a cleaning spray and paper towels.

Then I bring all my **toys** upstairs. Sometimes I put them in a bag first so they're easier to carry.

Next we **sanitize** the baby toys by putting them in a little machine for ten minutes.

I put all my Nintendo **games** and my LEGOs back where they belong.

I help **vacuum** the rug and furniture with a small, handheld vacuum.

Finally, I help **load** the dishwasher and the washing machine.

Phew! All done!

What kind of chores do you do to help your family?

Now It's . . .
Family Time!

I love my family!

Meow!

Meet my pet cats!

We have two cats. Their names are **Mr. Scratchy** and **Pebbles**. I got them as a surprise Christmas present last year! My daddy adopted them from a shelter when they were babies. At first he was only going to get one cat, but then he learned that the cat had a brother. So we got two cats! They are about two years old.

Mr. Scratchy is a dark gray cat, and Pebbles is light gray with a white belly and paws.

At first the cats were a little scared. Everything in our house was new to them—including me and my sisters! But then the cats started playing with the **toys** we got them. Mr. Scratchy was more outgoing. Pebbles was a little bit shy. But before we knew it, they

Pebbles

Mr. Scratchy

were purring and happy and sitting on my lap!

Once we had pet cats, we needed a few supplies. We went to the pet store and picked out furry **beds** for them. Cats don't need blankets because they have fur.

We also picked up kitty **litter boxes** and a **scratching post** they can climb.

Now that the cats feel comfortable in our home, they are always fighting each other on the floor—it's like they're playing warriors or soldiers or something.

Pebbles likes to look out the window. Sometimes Mr. Scratchy will bother him because he wants to play instead.

My sisters also like playing with our pet cats a lot! When we first got them, my sisters were so excited. They thought the cats were so cute that they **screamed**.

6:00 p.m. Drawing Time!

It might seem like I'm making videos all the time, but really it's a small part of my life. When I'm not making YouTube videos, I'm reading, **drawing**, playing with LEGOs, playing video games, or doing puzzles.

Look at this picture I drew!

6:30 p.m. *Dinnertime!*

I love eating dinner with my family. We talk about our days. Tonight my parents and sisters have **a few questions** for me:

Q: What do you want to be when you grow up?

Q: If you could have a superpower, what would it be?

44

Q: If you could invite a famous person on your show, who would it be?

A: I love gaming and would love to meet EthanGamer.

A: A game developer.

A: Flying.

It's almost time to get ready for bed. But first let's play a game of **Would You Rather**! My answers are highlighted in yellow below. What about you? What would you pick?

Would you rather . . .

tell the truth ↖or↗ do a dare?

swim in a pool ↖or↗ swim in the ocean?

live on the moon ↖or↗ live under the sea?

be able to read minds ↖or↗ have X-ray vision?

go back in time ↖or↗ go into the future?

stand forever ↖or↗ sit forever?

eat ice cream for every meal ↖or↗ eat candy for every meal?

eat all your vegetables every day ↖or↗ take a bath every day?

stay up late ↖or↗ get up early?

have hair that sticks up all the time ↖or↗ have no hair at all?

WAKE UP!

Sometimes It's Just Silly Time!

49

When Is It Filming Time?

You might be wondering when I film my videos. I don't film every day. I usually make my videos over the weekend, during my sisters' naptimes. I make all kinds of videos! I've reviewed a lot of toys on my channel, but some of my favorite ones to play with are Spider-Man and Batman action figures. I also love LEGOs, of course!

I watch other people's videos on YouTube too. My favorite videos to watch are EthanGamer, EvanTubeHD, and *Roblox* gaming videos.

I love my iPad, but my parents limit my screen time. I have thirty minutes on weekdays and one hour on Saturdays and Sundays.

I have a new gaming channel called **VTubers**! On my channel, we review video games of all kinds.

The *V* in VTubers stands for **"virtual."** When something is virtual, it means it's simulated on a computer—**it's not real**! I collaborate with fun, virtual characters on this channel.

Because my family and I like gaming so much, we actually have a special **gaming room** where we play and film our videos. In our gaming room we have a giant computer, gaming systems like Wii U and PlayStation 4, a giant TV, lots of games, and of course cameras.

We also have lights and a green screen, which lets us change the background of our videos really easily. That's how we make it look like we've teleported to a different location. It's all virtual!

In my first episode of VTubers, I played Hide and Seek on *Roblox* with Combo Panda. I love making dual gaming videos, where you can watch two people playing the same game together.

In my next episode, I played *Kirby Star Allies* with Daddy. We finished the demo version. The game wasn't even out yet!

7:30 p.m. *Bathtime!*

Now it's time to take a **bath**. In the bath, I like to play with monster trucks and cars.

After my bath, I put on my pajamas, and then Daddy and I play a **video game** for thirty minutes. My little sisters watch.

Sometimes, before bed, I drink some medicine because I have seasonal allergies. Then I take my **vitamin** gummies.

Then it's time to **brush my teeth**!

Before bed, I play a **board game** or a **card game** with Mommy. Sometimes one of my sisters will play with us if she hasn't fallen asleep yet.

Finally, at about eight thirty p.m., we pick out a book to read.

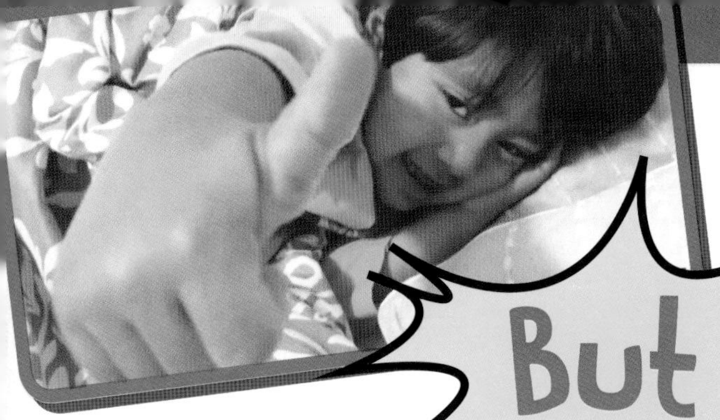

Today was an awesome day!

But

if I could spend a day doing whatever I wanted, I would ...

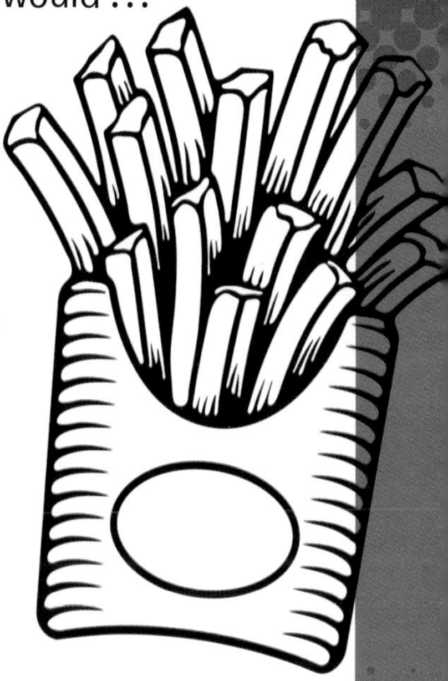

Eat French fries all day.

Watch my favorite YouTubers.

Drink milk—it's my favorite type of drink!

Build LEGOs.

Play Roblox.

Milk

What would you do if you could spend a day doing whatever you wanted?

I'm getting sleepy . . . I can tell because I'm yawning!

Do you know why you yawn?

Your brain is like a computer. When it works hard, it warms up. Playing video games, being active, and thinking is hard work for your brain. Your brain needs a break every so often.

You yawn because your brain needs to cool off. When you yawn, you can breathe in more air. That air helps your brain cool down. And that's why you yawn!

Yawning isn't just for humans. Animals yawn too. Cats, dogs, snakes, fish—they all yawn.

Now it's time for bed.
I wonder what I'll dream about tonight. Maybe it'll be a peek into my future?

Maybe I'll dream about when I'm twelve years old, and I'm making **gaming videos** for my gaming channel on YouTube. We just started it, and I'd like to grow the channel even more! There are so many video games out there that I'd like to play.

Maybe I'll dream about when I'm twenty-two years old and I'm a **video editor**. That's someone who makes cool videos. I am inspired by the cool animation and virtual stuff that my family makes today. It would be fun to still make videos as an adult!

ZZZ

Yawning really is contagious. That means if you see someone yawn, it might make you yawn too.

Are you yawning yet?

55

Good night!

Thanks for following me through my day.
See you again on my channel for more fun!

How well do you know Ryan?
Take the ULTIMATE
Ryan ToysReview Quiz
on page 216.

"HobbyPig is silly and HobbyFrog is smart!"
—HobbyBear

"If I had to pick one word to describe my brothers, I'd say HobbyFrog is 'creative' and HobbyBear is 'feisty.'"
—HobbyPig

"And if I had to pick one word for HobbyPig, it would be 'comedy.'"
—HobbyFrog

Hi! We're the Hobbykids!

You probably know us from our YouTube channel, **HobbykidsTV**. You can call us by our nicknames: **HobbyPig**, **HobbyFrog**, and **HobbyBear**. We are three brothers who like to make funny videos.

When I was five, I loved Angry Birds. I loved the pigs because they were green, and it was my favorite color. So it was easy to pick my name: **HobbyPig!**

I loved jumping in my jumper when I was a baby. I could stay in there for hours! So my parents called me Frog for years. That's why I'm **HobbyFrog!**

Mom and Dad called me HobbyBaby for a while because I was so little. But then we decided **HobbyBear** was a better name because I'm a little bossy and I have big paws—er, hands!

HobbyPig's Favorite . . .

> I can make anyone laugh!

Ice cream flavor:

mint chocolate chip

Food: chicken

Sport: catch

Animal: pig

Season: fall

Color: green

Soda: root beer

Number: 7

Emoji: 💩

Place to visit: Disneyland

Superhero: me (J/K!)

Hobby: making videos

Age: I'm the oldest!
Height: taller than a pig
Hair color: brown
Eye color: brown

"HobbyPig can gather a crowd. I don't know how he does it!" —HobbyMom

HobbyFrog's Favorite . . .

My hidden talents are sketching and painting!

Ice cream flavor: strawberry

Food: Pizza Hut

Sport: swimming

Animal: frog

Season: summer

Color: red

Soda: root beer

Number: 8

Emoji:

Place to visit: Legoland

Superhero: Cyborg

Hobby: Building LEGOs

Age: I'm the middle brother!
Height: taller than a frog
Hair color: blond
Eye color: blue

"HobbyFrog is so talented when it comes to art and creativity—he's like a little engineer." —HobbyDad

HobbyBear's Favorite . . .

I love to help!

Ice cream flavor: chocolate

Foods: pizza and chicken

Sport: baseball

Animal: bear

Season: summer

Color: blue

Soda: Orange Crush

Number: 6

Emoji:

Place to visit: Legoland

Superhero: the Hulk

Hobby: making videos

Age: I'm the youngest!
Height: shorter than a bear
Hair color: blond
Eye color: green

"His imagination is so huge. HobbyBear is always up for an adventure!"
—HobbyMom

Ice cream flavor
Frog: strawberry ☑
Bear: chocolate ☑

Both correct! Plus 2 points!

Food
Frog: strawberries ☐
Bear: pizza ☑

One correct! Plus 1 point!

Subject in school
Frog: science ☑
Bear: spelling ☐

One correct! Plus 1 point!

Sport
Frog: catch ☐
Bear: wrestling ☐

Both wrong. No points!

Animal
Frog: frog ☑
Bear: bear ☑

Both correct! Plus 2 points!

Color
Frog: red ☑
Bear: blue ☑

Both correct! Plus 2 points!

Soda
Frog: root beer ☑
Bear: root beer ☐

One correct! Plus 1 point!

Number
Frog: 0 ☐
Bear: 1 ☐

Both wrong. No points!

Emoji
Frog: 💩 ☐
Bear: 💩 ☐

Both wrong. No points!

Costume to dress up in
Frog: Bumblebee Transformer ☑
Bear: Batman ☐

One correct! Plus 1 point!

Hobby
Frog: filming ☐
Bear: wrestling HobbyPig ☐

Both wrong. No points!

Playground activity
Frog: swing ☐
Bear: swing ☐

Both wrong. No points!

HobbyPig has 10 points!

Next, I tried to guess **HobbyPig**'s and **HobbyBear**'s favorites. Did I get a good score?

Ice cream flavor
Pig: vanilla ☐
Bear: chocolate ☑

One correct! Plus 1 point!

Food
Pig: taquitos ☐
Bear: pizza ☑

One correct! Plus 1 point!

Subject in school
Pig: science ☐
Bear: reading ☐

Both wrong. No points!

Sport
Pig: boxing ☐
Bear: boxing ☐

Both wrong. No points!

Animal
Pig: pig ☑
Bear: bear ☑

Both correct! Plus 2 points!

Color
Pig: green ☑
Bear: blue ☑

Both correct! Plus 2 points!

Soda
Pig: root beer ☑
Bear: Sprite ☐

One correct! Plus 1 point!

Number
Pig: 9 ☐
Bear: 5 ☐

Both wrong. No points!

Emoji
Pig: 🐷 ☐
Bear: 🐻 ☑

One correct! Plus 1 point!

Costume to dress up in
Pig: Grimlock ☐
Bear: Spider-Man ☑

One correct! Plus 1 point!

Hobby
Pig: Roblox ☐
Bear: movies ☐

Both wrong. No points!

Playground activity
Pig: rock wall ☐
Bear: slide ☑

One correct! Plus 1 point!

HobbyFrog has 10 points!

65

Ice cream flavor
Pig: lemon ☐
Frog: strawberry ☑

One correct! Plus 1 point!

Food
Pig: chicken ☑
Frog: pancakes with strawberries ☐

One correct! Plus 1 point!

Subject in school
Pig: not sure ☐
Frog: not sure ☐

Both wrong. No points!

Sport
Pig: soccer ☐
Frog: basketball ☐

Both wrong. No points!

Animal
Pig: pig ☑
Frog: frog ☑

Both correct! Plus 2 points!

Color
Pig: green ☑
Frog: red ☑

Both correct! Plus 2 points!

Soda
Pig: smoothie ☐
Frog: water ☐

Both wrong. No points!

Number
Pig: 6 ☐
Frog: 4 ☐

Both wrong. No points!

Emoji
Pig: 🐷 ☐
Frog: 🐸 ☑

One correct! Plus 1 point!

Costume to dress up in
Pig: pig ☐
Frog: frog ☐

Both wrong. No points!

Hobby
Pig: roller coaster ☐
Frog: rodeo ☐

Both wrong. No points!

Playground activity
Pig: swing ☑
Frog: slide ☑

Both correct! Plus 2 points!

HobbyBear has 9 points!

Which BROTHER knows his SIBLINGS best?

HobbyPig: 10 points
HobbyFrog: 10 points
HobbyBear: 9 points

It's a tie between HobbyPig and HobbyFrog! Here's the

TIEBREAKER ROUND!

HobbyPig, tell us your brothers' favorite place that they've been:

Frog: Legoland ☑
Bear: Legoland ☑

Both correct! Plus 2 points!

HobbyFrog, tell us your brothers' favorite place that they've been:

Pig: the mall ☐
Bear: museum ☐

Both wrong. No points!

RESULT:

What a close one! HobbyPig wins with 12 points! Congrats, HobbyPig!

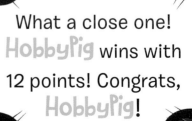

Watch Us!

How We Got Started

We liked watching YouTube videos, but when we got started there weren't a lot of channels just for kids. We knew we could make something even better. So we tried it out. And it worked! We love making kids happy, and we like that our channel teaches kids stuff. We get to show kids how stuff works.

Our First Videos

You know those little eggs with tiny toy surprises in them? We had a great idea about making the **world's biggest surprise egg**. It had never been done before. We started making those videos and they went viral because no one had ever seen them before.

WANT TO START A YOUTUBE PAGE WITH YOUR FAMILY? HERE ARE SOME OF OUR TIPS.

🔊 Keep filming fun. We always try to film something that's fun for all three of us. We are all very different, but we all have a fun time if the video has something exciting for each person.

🔊 Do what you like! Follow your interests. If you're really into Pokémon then make Pokémon videos. Just do whatever your interests are!

Q: Who do you like watching on YouTube?

A: We like DanTDM, stampylonghead, iBallisticSquid, and Larva TUBA.

Inside HobbyKidsTV

SUBSCRIBERS: 3 million+

UPLOADING SINCE: May 2013

TOTAL VIEWS: 5.7 billion+

OTHER CHANNELS: HobbyFamilyTV, HobbykidsGaming, HobbyPigTV, HobbyFrogTV, HobbyBearTV, HobbykidsJR, HobbyMomTV, HobbyFoodTV

Our Most-Watched Videos

Some of our videos have been watched as many as fifty-four million times! Sometimes the most popular one changes every week.

One of our most popular videos is "Giant Superman Egg Adventure." We found lots of giant surprise eggs and helped save Superman from kryptonite!

Another popular video is "Giant Slinky Surprise Egg." There was a rainbow slinky so big that HobbyBear could fit inside it!

Q: What do you think about millions of people watching you?

A: I like entertaining them!

Our Messiest Video Ever!

In the "Giant JELLO Surprise Egg!" video, we filled an inflatable pool in our backyard with strawberry gelatin. It took lots of boxes of gelatin powder and a hose to fill it up. When we stepped into the pool, we could barely move. It felt weird. Very gooey. (We would totally do it again, though!) Even though the Jell-O felt cold, we sat in it, found the hidden toys, and even threw some gelatin at each other, which got all over our yard. When it was time to clean up, the gelatin filled three trash cans!

Sometimes our videos get messy! And you can tell if you see our driveway. Sometimes there's chalk everywhere, plus Spider-Man Silly String that will probably stay stuck there for eternity.

Q: Do you get along with your siblings off camera?

A: Yes. We're the same on camera and off camera.

What It's Really Like to Be on YouTube

Here's something other kids should know if they want to start their own channel: **getting views is very hard**! But if you're smart and creative with your own ideas, you'll do a great job. We wish we had more time to make videos because we have so much fun.

When Things Go Wrong

Not everything goes perfectly when we film a video. One time we filmed a **"Giant *Finding Dory* Surprise Egg"** video, but when we watched it afterward, the video had no audio. That means that after we filmed, you could see everything but you couldn't hear anything. What a bummer! Other times we've had the audio work but no video.

Our fans are so great. The comments that they leave us keep us going, and we can't wait to keep making more videos for them.

Q: How many videos have you uploaded?

A: Close to 3,000 on HobbyKidsTV

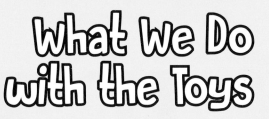

What We Do with the Toys

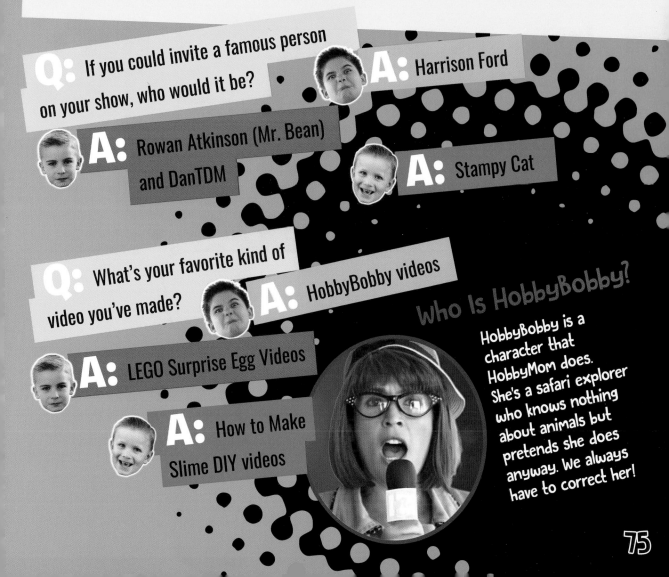

A lot of our videos are filled with toys and products. **But there's no way we keep all the things we review.** We donate them to charity. We only pick a couple of things we love to keep in our bedrooms, like Nerf Blasters and lightsabers. We're big Star Wars fans!

Q: If you could invite a famous person on your show, who would it be?

A: Harrison Ford

A: Rowan Atkinson (Mr. Bean) and DanTDM

A: Stampy Cat

Q: What's your favorite kind of video you've made?

A: HobbyBobby videos

A: LEGO Surprise Egg Videos

A: How to Make Slime DIY videos

Who Is HobbyBobby?

HobbyBobby is a character that HobbyMom does. She's a safari explorer who knows nothing about animals but pretends she does anyway. We always have to correct her!

A Day in Our Lives

Good morning!

Our parents, **HobbyMom** and **HobbyDad**, are already awake. Do you want to get to know them?

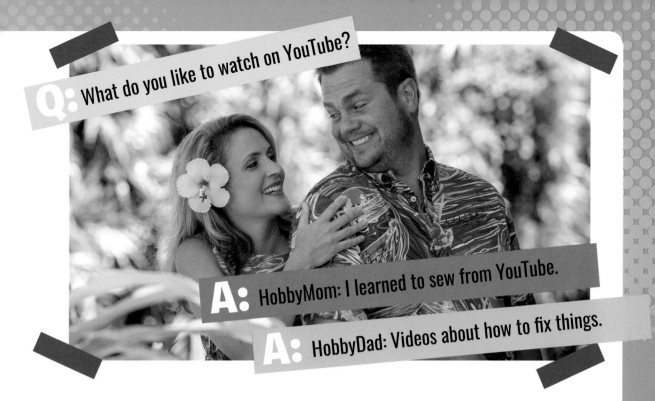

Q: What do you like to watch on YouTube?

A: HobbyMom: I learned to sew from YouTube.

A: HobbyDad: Videos about how to fix things.

Our mom and dad both love being YouTubers. They first started posting ten years ago, when HobbyPig was a baby and snorting like a piglet. Now they work hard and help us **make fun videos**.

HobbyMom

HobbyDad

The beautiful testimonials we get daily from parents bring us so much joy.

We couldn't do it without our kids. Our boys are a big part of the creative process and we're really proud of them.

After saying good morning, we brush our teeth. Then we eat **BREAKFAST**.

HobbyPig: I eat a bowl of Honey Nut Cheerios.

HobbyFrog: I eat a peanut butter and jelly sandwich.

HobbyBear: I eat slippery bacon. That means no crispy pieces!

Slippery!

79

Then we say good morning to **Flappy**. He's our pet dog!

He's a Chiweenie, which means he's half Chihuahua and half Dachshund, so he's a hot-dog dog.

He's still just a puppy—one year old.

He's actually a really cool color, like a red color.

His ears are hilarious. They flap like Dumbo's.

It's . . . Flappy!

When we first got Flappy, he was so little—only two months old!

Right away, he was really nice and very snuggly. It was hard to hold him because he was so **squiggly** and **squirmy**.

Then he wanted to play. He licked our feet and jumped up our legs like, "Hey, play with me!"

Before we could take him home, we had to pick out toys, bowls, food, a dog bed, and more.

At home, we gave him a bath in our bathroom sink. He was so tiny that he fit just fine.

After his bath, he fell asleep right on HobbyPig's chest. It was so sweet!

In **art class** we have an assignment to draw whatever we want. Can you guess what we drew?

A DRAWING BY HOBBYPIG.

A DRAWING BY HOBBYFROG.

A DRAWING BY **HOBBYBEAR**.

After school, we do our **homework**. We get an allowance, but we have to do **chores** to earn it.

We help our parents with things like **cleaning up** the doggy doo, **unloading** the groceries, **bringing** laundry to the washer, and **tidying** the living room.

We **wipe off the kitchen counters** with cleaning spray and paper towels.

We **load water bottles** into the fridge. Even **HobbyBear** can do that!

If we **find trash** on the floor, we pick it up and put it in the bin. Then HobbyPig takes the trash outside—or else it will stink!

HEY, HOBBYPIG, DON'T FORGET TO PUT A NEW BAG IN THE TRASH BIN!

Sometimes HobbyPig helps me with my homework.

Chores are important because you're helping your family. But it's not our favorite thing ever (especially taking the trash outside, because it stinks!). If we could have a **PERFECT DAY**, we definitely wouldn't be doing chores.

HobbyPig: My best day ever would mean playing **lots of video games** and eating **lots of potato chips**!

HobbyFrog: All I'd want to do is **build LEGO sets**. I would go to **Legoland** because there are millions of LEGOs you can build with in the main lobby of the hotel.

HobbyBear: I'd play **Minecraft**, **paint**, and then **play with the puppy**. Or sit on the couch **watching movies** with my brothers.

At the end of the day, we'd all watch *SpongeBob SquarePants*.

We also help out by going grocery shopping with our parents. There's always a lot to buy because we're a big family! Here are some of the things we like to buy at the grocery store.

- ☐ corn
- ☐ peas
- ☐ broccoli
- ☐ baby carrots
- ☐ avocado
- ☐ pineapples
- ☐ mandarin oranges
- ☐ mangoes
- ☐ bananas
- ☐ raspberries
- ☐ apples
- ☐ applesauce
- ☐ bread
- ☐ crackers
- ☐ rice cakes

- ☐ peanut butter
- ☐ tortilla chips and salsa
- ☐ black beans
- ☐ popcorn
- ☐ gum
- ☐ M&M'S
- ☐ milk
- ☐ yogurt
- ☐ nuts
- ☐ beef jerky
- ☐ turkey dogs
- ☐ chicken
- ☐ shrimp
- ☐ crab legs
- ☐ water bottles

We like to push our own small shopping carts around the store because it's fun. But make sure you don't crash into anyone!

Maybe we'll see a fan at the store. We've had fans say hi in public bathrooms, doctors' offices, in the security line at the airport, on the plane . . . lots of places!

It's fun when we get recognized by fans. We like it, and it makes us happy. They usually say, **"YOU'RE THE HOBBYKIDS!"** Then they start asking us questions.

Q: What's the one question you always get asked by your fans?

A: "Are you real?"

Q: What's the craziest question you've ever been asked?

A: "Can you live with me?"

Q: What's a fan question that you can't answer?

A: "What are your real names?"

We love you, fans! Work hard. Have fun.

On the way home from the grocery store, we play a game of **Would You Rather**.

The three of us are very different, but we agreed on almost all the answers! What would you pick?

Our answers are highlighted in blue below.

Would you rather . . .

tell the truth ↖or↗ do a dare ?∗

∗HobbyFrog says "truth" and HobbyPig says "dare"!

swim in a pool ↖or↗ swim in the ocean?

live on the moon ↖or↗ live under the sea?

be able to read minds ↖or↗ have X-ray vision?

go back in time ↖or↗ go into the future?

have a pet vampire bat ↖or↗ have a pet slug?

stand forever ↖or↗ sit forever?

eat ice cream for every meal ↖or↗ eat candy for every meal?

eat all your vegetables every day ↖or↗ take a bath every day?

stay up late ↖or↗ get up early?

have hair that sticks up all the time ↖or↗ have no hair at all?

5:00 p.m. *Time for Fun!*

Once we're done with school, homework, and chores, it's time for fun! We have fun playing with Flappy, riding our bikes, and swimming.

I like to make videos, play with Nerf guns, and play *Roblox* or *Minecraft*. I also love comedy movies and funny YouTube videos where people slip and fall.

I like to build LEGOs and draw. If I want to do something outside, I'll play on the swing set. If I'm looking to laugh, all I have to do is play with HobbyPig. When we play together, he does hilarious stuff.

I like painting and making arts and crafts. I also like watching movies.

But Most of All, We Love

Being Silly!

CROSS EYES!

FISH FACE!

SO SOUR!

6:00 p.m. Dinnertime!

Today we get to eat some of our favorite foods for dinner!

I like to eat chips and salsa.

I like to eat spaghetti.

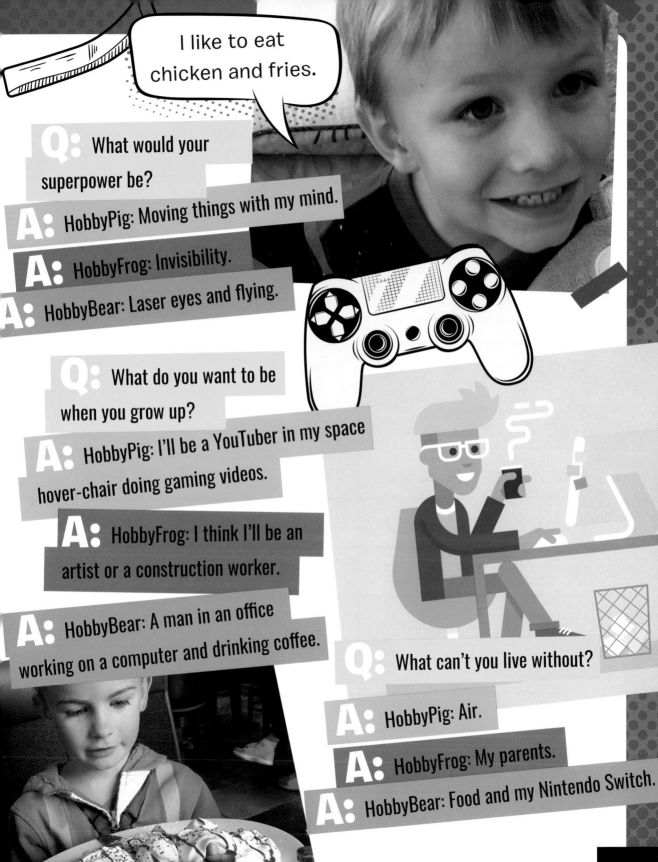

I like to eat chicken and fries.

Q: What would your superpower be?

A: HobbyPig: Moving things with my mind.

A: HobbyFrog: Invisibility.

A: HobbyBear: Laser eyes and flying.

Q: What do you want to be when you grow up?

A: HobbyPig: I'll be a YouTuber in my space hover-chair doing gaming videos.

A: HobbyFrog: I think I'll be an artist or a construction worker.

A: HobbyBear: A man in an office working on a computer and drinking coffee.

Q: What can't you live without?

A: HobbyPig: Air.

A: HobbyFrog: My parents.

A: HobbyBear: Food and my Nintendo Switch.

After dinner, we play a game of **Cool or Drool**. We tried to get Flappy to play too, but we're not sure he understood the game. . . .

HERE ARE OUR ANSWERS!

	HobbyPig	HobbyFrog	HobbyBear	Flappy
Rainbows	cool*	cool	cool	Woof!
Video games	cool	cool	cool	Woof!
Hedgehogs	cool	drool	cool	Woof!
Unicorns	amazing!	cool	cool	Woof!
Balloons	cool	cool	cool	Woof!
Snow	cool	cool	cool	Woof!
The beach	drool	cool	cool	Woof!
Pirates	cool	cool	drool	Woof!

* (because unicorns fart them)

	HobbyPig	HobbyFrog	HobbyBear	Flappy
Candy corn	cool	cool	cool	woof!
Scary stories	drool	drool	drool	woof!
Slime	cool	cool	cool	woof!
Boogers	cool	drool	drool	woof!
Pizza	cool	cool	cool	woof!
Bugs	drool	cool	drool	woof!
Dinosaurs	cool	cool	cool	woof!

After the game, we find **HobbyMom** putting our family photos into a **PHOTO ALBUM**. There are a lot of photos, even ones from when we were babies!

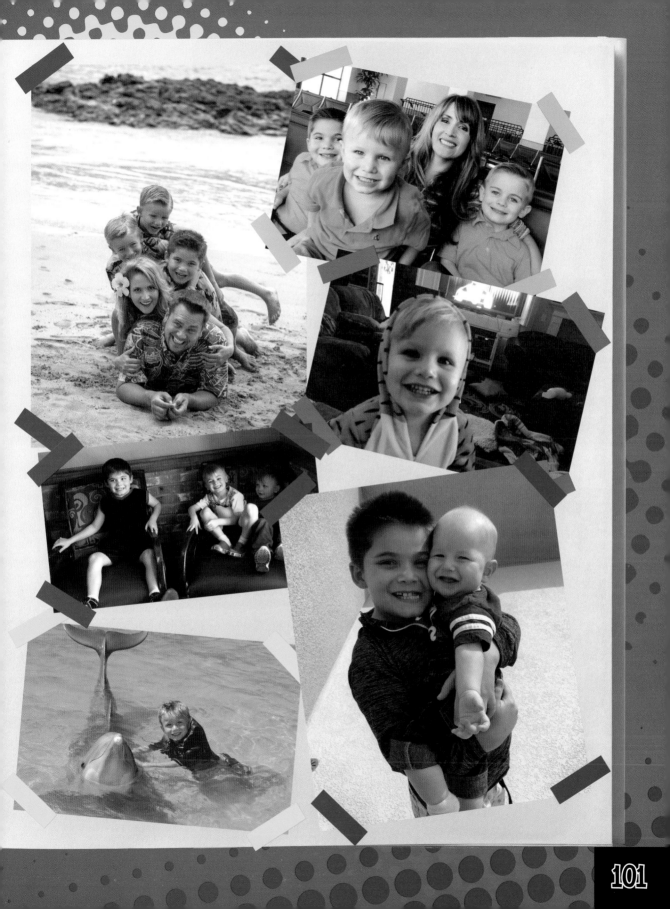

Now we each take a bath before bed.

BUBBLE BATHS!

Maybe there will be a **surprise egg** in the tub. Once we filmed a video that had a giant surprise egg in the bathtub! (Don't worry, we kept our swimsuits on!)

Our first surprise was bubble bath. We made bubble beards and hair—hilarious!

Then we opened up a bunch of bath toys that float, swim, or stick to the sides of the tub.

We even got some **crayons** that were especially made for the bathtub. That meant **HobbyMom** allowed us to write on the walls and the sides of the tub! It was okay, though, because it all washed off.

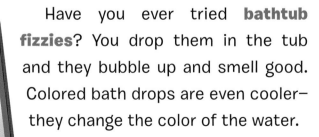

Have you ever tried **bathtub fizzies**? You drop them in the tub and they bubble up and smell good. Colored bath drops are even cooler—they change the color of the water.

We also got some shampoo and body wash that smelled good. **HobbyBear** poured way too much onto HobbyPig's hair. **His hair was extra clean that day!**

Wouldn't you be much more excited to take a bath if there was a surprise egg waiting for you every time?

OH! WE JUST THOUGHT OF A COOL IDEA FOR OUR NEXT VIDEO!

We come up with some of our best ideas at the dinner table or at other random times, like when we're driving in the car or taking baths. We always keep our eyes open for ideas, and they just pop up in our heads. Our parents keep notepads everywhere so they can write down all our ideas. We like to be different!

What's the idea, you ask? That's a secret until the video gets uploaded to our channel!

9:00 p.m. *Bedtime!*

Good night! Thanks for joining us today. We hope you had fun! See you again on our channel!

How well do you know the Hobbykids? Take the ULTIMATE HobbykidsTV Quiz on page 218.

105

A Day with Jillian

from JillianTubeHD™

Hi! I'm Jillian!

Age: 10
Height: 54½ inches
(about 4½ feet)
Hair color: brown
Eye color: brown

Q: What's one word that describes you?

A: "Athletic."

I'm Jillian from JillianTubeHD! I have my own YouTube channel, where I post vlogs, toy reviews, music videos, crafts, and more things that I like to do. I also appear in a lot of videos with my older brother, Evan, on his channel.

Read all about my brother, Evan, in his section, which starts on page 161!

My Favorite . . .

Ice cream flavor: peppermint

Food: mashed potatoes with no skin

Subject: math

Movie: *The Greatest Showman*

Animal: I love horses!

Book: *Charlie and the Chocolate Factory*

Place to visit: Hawaii

Holiday: Christmas

Season: summer

Colors: magenta and teal

Drink: Dr Pepper

Number: 8

Emoji:

Hobby: singing

Superhero: Wonder Woman

Watch Me!

TA-DA!

My First Video

I have a lot of "first" videos depending on what you mean! If you look at the oldest video on my channel, it's a video of me as a baby. I'm learning how to walk! Obviously, I wasn't posting videos on YouTube while I was still wearing diapers. It's a flashback video.

You have to go to EvanTubeHD to watch my first solo video for YouTube. It's seriously so cute. Evan had allergies, so I filmed the video for him. I'm only three years old, I have pigtail braids, and you can barely understand what I'm saying sometimes. I talk about the female Angry Birds clay models that my dad made. I'm also wearing Angry Birds pajamas that I'm really excited about.

MY FIRST VIDEOS!

How I Got Started

My brother, Evan, started making YouTube videos when he was five years old. At first I would just appear in his videos (the first one was a Christmas present video and I was so little!), but then I started making videos of my own.

My favorite kinds of videos to make are **craft** ones because I get to experiment with things. Sometimes I don't even use measurements! I just pour stuff in. I like to try craft kits too. They are fun.

Q: What do you think about millions of people watching you?

A: It's cool that so many people want to watch our videos.

MERRY CHRISTMAS

MY DEBUT ON YOUTUBE!

Inside

JillianTubeHD

SUBSCRIBERS: 1.2 million+

UPLOADING SINCE: January 2016

TOTAL VIEWS: 300 million+

My Longest Video

Some videos take only twenty minutes to film, but one video took four days! We shot a little bit each day. It was an Enchantimals video, and my dog, Chloe, was in the video too. But it was hard to get her to cooperate. It was a cute skit, but it was also really hot during filming, so we didn't want to go outside. It was worth it in the end, though. The video came out great!

My Messiest Video Ever!

Sometimes our challenge videos can get really messy, but the messiest moment was when a bottle of pancake batter exploded all over the place. Evan and I were doing a Pancake Art Challenge, and I think one of the bottles had too much batter in it. When I opened it up, the batter splattered on Evan. It was pretty funny. We put the video in slow motion, and Evan's face was so hilarious.

My Favorite Video

My favorite video is the "Eat It or Wear It Challenge." I liked watching the video afterward. It was funny to watch back but not so funny to film. I was getting things dumped on my head! I love to get messy, though. When we were done filming, we hosed ourselves off then took quick showers.

How to Do the
Eat It or Wear It Challenge

You'll need two players for this game. Ask an adult to put different kinds of food—some good, some bad—in paper bags labeled with numbers. Then take turns opening a bag. Your option is to eat or wear the food inside the bag! If you eat it, you have to eat one big spoonful, but then you get to dump the leftovers on the other player's head. Play outside because it gets messy fast!

Another Fun Challenge

I also like the Pie Face Challenge. There is a game called Pie Face, and it comes with a spinner and a whipped-cream-flinging contraption. Players take turns turning the handle however many times the spinner tells them to. You never know whose turn will trigger the whipped cream to fly at their face!

We like this challenge so much that we had our parents try it too. When Evan and I played, Evan kept flinching because he was so scared that he'd get hit with whipped cream. My dad was the same way, but my mom got hit first! It even got in her hair. My parents are so crazy that they added chocolate syrup on top of the whipped cream. Then my dad got hit on the first twist!

A Day in My Life

Mon	Tue	Wed	Thu	Fri	Sat	Sun

Good morning!

I like to sleep in because I go to sleep really late, so Mom wakes me up in the morning. It's also hard to leave my bedroom and get ready for school because I love my bed so much! I sleep with a lot of stuffed animals, dolls, and pillows.

I have a bunk bed with a desk under it, and a big pink beanbag chair right next to it.

There are three bins of stuffed animals under my desk!

My doll collection is on display too.

I like **UNICORNS.** I have a unicorn head that sticks out of the wall in my room, and I can hang my stuff on it.

I also have a **BEAR** that's really, really big. He's humongous, and my uncle gave him to me. I call him **Big Bear**. He's my favorite!

Once I finally get out of bed, I eat **breakfast**. Sometimes I eat cereal, and other times I eat waffles with Nutella.

After breakfast, I go upstairs and get dressed and brush my teeth. I usually forget my socks!

I also brush my hair, which is starting to get long again. **I've donated my hair to Locks of Love twice.** Locks of Love makes wigs out of donated hair and gives them to children who have lost their own hair because of a medical condition.

When you donate your hair, the stylist puts your hair in a ponytail and then *snip, snip!* It feels so short once it gets cut—that's because at least ten inches of hair gets cut. The last time I donated, I couldn't even put my hair up in a ponytail afterward! But that's okay because I'll just grow it out again.

8:00 a.m. *Time for School!*

Now it's time for school. Math class is my favorite part of the day.

Sometimes we have to do reports and projects in class. Once I did a presentation where I dressed up as Wilbur Wright. He and his brother, Orville, built the first airplane in 1903. To dress up like him, I had to borrow Evan's clothes. I wonder what our next project will be!

For lunch, I usually bring my own food. **Soup, Jell-O**, and **fruit** are my favorites.

My favorite kind of books are . . . fiction books. That's what I mostly read, but I read some nonfiction too. One of my favorite books is *Charlie and the Chocolate Factory*.

During lunch, my friends dare me to play a game of **Would You Rather**! My answers are highlighted in yellow below. What about you?

X-RAY VISION

Would you rather . . .

tell the truth ↖or↗ do a dare ?

swim in a pool ↖or↗ swim in the ocean ?

live on the moon ↖or↗ live under the sea ?

be able to read minds ↖or↗ have X-ray vision ?

go back in time ↖or↗ go into the future ?* I don't want to see my future, I want to live it!

stand forever ↖or↗ sit forever ?

eat ice cream ↖or↗ eat candy
for every meal   for every meal?* But only if it wouldn't
                                            make me sick!

eat all your vegetables ↖or↗ take a bath
                               every day?*   I love vegetables!

stay up late ↖or↗ get up early?

have hair that sticks ↖or↗ have no hair at all?
up all the time

Life with Braces

In September 2017 I got braces! Just on the top teeth, though.

Why Did I Need Braces?

My mouth was a little crowded. I had a big gap in my front teeth that they needed to close up so other adult teeth could come in. I need to keep my braces on for a year and a half, then wait for all my baby teeth to fall out. Then I get a full set of braces on. It's a process!

What It Was Like to Get Braces

I was kind of nervous and had a lot of stomachaches the day I got my braces. My mom was kind of nervous too because she never had braces. But my dad had them twice!

The first thing I did at the orthodontist's office was brush my teeth really well. I brought a blanket to keep myself warm while they worked on my teeth. They made me wear these sunglasses to protect my eyes. Then I opened my mouth and they got to work!

They stuck a lot of things in my mouth, then started gluing on each individual brace. Then I got to choose the color of my elastics. I chose pink! They threaded the wire through the braces, then added the elastics.

It didn't hurt and it didn't take that long. But by the end of the day, my teeth started hurting a bit. We got frozen yogurt and that made me feel better!

Taking Care of My Teeth

The orthodontist showed me how to brush my teeth now that I have braces. I have to brush under, on, and above my braces instead of just across the front of my teeth. I got a new electric toothbrush to make sure my teeth stay healthy. I'm supposed to brush three times a day.

I also have to remember to not eat hard or chewy foods. I can't eat things like popcorn, nuts, hard candy, chewing gum, and sticky candy like caramel. Boo!

What's an orthodontist? An orthodontist is a special type of dentist who can straighten crooked teeth!

3:30 p.m. *Dance Time!*

I'm involved in a lot of activities. I have **tap classes** and **Zumba** . . . plus piano!

What Is Tap Dance?

Tap dance is a kind of dance that's all about the footwork. You wear special shoes with taps on the heel and toe. When the taps hit the floor, they make a cool sound! I only wear my tap shoes in dance class. I'd never wear them on the sidewalk or at school.

What Is Zumba?

Zumba is like an intense dance workout. During the class, you learn a routine to a song and then perform it. You sweat a lot, but it's really fun! And whenever that song comes on the radio, you'll know a cool dance to perform.

JILLIAN'S DANCE TIPS

🔊 **ALWAYS SMILE!** Keep your chin up and a smile on your face while you are performing.

🔊 **DON'T GIVE UP!** The only way you can get better is if you keep practicing. You'll get it eventually.

🔊 **TRY NEW THINGS.** Tap and Zumba are very different, but there are things I like about each one. You never know until you try!

I also take **voice lessons,** and I'm in a **choir**, too!

Singing is my favorite activity, but sometimes I get nervous when I have to sing a solo in my choir or at a recital.

I sang the national anthem at one of the football games near us when I was nine years old. I was scared because it was my first time singing the national anthem. I sang from the press box, so not everyone could see me, but I could see them if I wanted to. Instead, I just looked at my voice teacher the whole time.

It went pretty well, except the microphone made a screeching noise for a little bit. I just kept singing! Then, when I came home, I sang the national anthem one more time for my family. At home I didn't have to worry about a microphone screeching.

JILLIAN'S SINGING TIPS

🔊 **PRACTICE!** Before I sang the national anthem, I practiced a lot. That's the only way to be prepared.

🔊 **DON'T WORRY!** Whether I'm singing to a big audience or singing on a YouTube video, I'm just trying to have fun.

🔊 **KEEP GOING!** Even if you mess up, just keep going. If the microphone screeches, just keep on singing like nothing happened.

Once my after-school activities are over, I come home and do my homework. There are some **chores** I have to do too.

Evan and I help out with **dishes**, take out the **garbage**, **tidy up**, and clean our bathroom. But we've **cleaned the toilet** only a few times.

4:30 p.m. Snack Time!

I'm usually hungry when I get home from my activities, so I eat a **snack** before dinner. Sometimes I make myself a **Banana S'mores Surprise!**

Do you want to learn how to make this snack? My mom and I decided it's a half-healthy snack, so it's not for every day. It's a little messy, so make sure you have some napkins.

Banana S'mores Surprise

You will need:

2 graham crackers

hazelnut spread

1 marshmallow

½ banana, sliced

butter knife for spreading

1. Start with two graham crackers. Add hazelnut spread onto the top of each cracker.

2. Add one marshmallow to the top of one graham cracker.

3. Put the cracker with the marshmallow on a plate and heat it in the microwave for 10 seconds.

4. Remove the plate from the microwave with an oven mitt, then add the second graham cracker (hazelnut spread side down) on top.

5. Now add more hazelnut spread on top of your s'more sandwich.

6. Add three banana slices on top.

NOW EAT!

DELICIOUS, RIGHT?

5:00 p.m. Filming Time!

When you hit one million subscribers, you get a Gold Play Button award from YouTube. That's why I made gold slime!

Sometimes Evan and I make videos after school, but we shoot mostly on the weekends when I have a lot of **energy**.

If you want to start a YouTube channel, I'd suggest making videos about **what you like**. For example, I like crafts and singing, so I make videos about that.

If the videos you make are a **big hit**, then I recommend you keep doing them. You can tell what your fans like based on the number of views and comments.

Q: Is there a place you'd never film?

A: The bathroom! Or my room when it is messy.

I know my fans really like when I make things like cookies. Or when I do a hairstyle. My video **"Rey Hair tutorial"** (from Star Wars) has more than seven million views!

I also love making slime. I love it so much that I had a slime party for my ninth birthday. My friends and I made fluffy slime, clear slime, glitter slime, and crunchy slime. And when I reached one million subscribers on my channel, I celebrated by making gold slime with my dad. And I didn't make just a little bit of slime, I made a *huge* batch.

Slime is really easy to make. Most of the ingredients are really simple, like glue and baking soda. You can find a lot of recipes online, but sometimes I don't use exact measurements. I just experiment until it feels nice and slimy!

Q: Do you film all the time?

A: Not all the time. But if we do something fun, we will try to record it.

Q: Do you have any superstitions about filming?

A: Don't film at three a.m. I'm usually asleep anyway, so I don't have to worry about that.

Q: Where do you get your ideas?

A: My family and my fans.

137

And don't forget, when you're filming . . .
ALWAYS HAVE FUN!

(I do!)

I Love My Fans!

If I could tell my fans anything, I would say, "Have fun" and "Thanks for watching!" Sometimes I read the comments with Dad. It's awesome to see what the fans say, like, "Oh, you have such a great singing voice."

Q: What's the craziest thing that's happened with a fan?

A: We met a kid on a cruise ship and then the same kid again in Hawaii.

Q: What's the one question you always get asked by your fans?

A: "Can we take a picture with you?"

Q: Do you ever get asked something you won't answer?

A: Yes! Things like "Where do you live?" and "What's your phone number?"

Q: Do you think about what to wear for each episode?

A: Most of the time Evan and I just wear what we had on during the day. Sometimes we have to look a certain way for the video. It just depends.

Q: Do you ever not feel like filming?

A: If I have a long day at school or I'm not feeling good, I don't film. So we just shoot on another day.

141

When I'm not filming an episode, I'm singing and dancing! **I also like to play with my dolls' hair.**

Here, I can show you how to do a **fishtail braid** with your doll's hair:

1. Start with your doll's hair in a ponytail.
2. Spread the ponytail into two parts.
3. Move a little bit of hair from the outside of the left side then cross it over and add it to the right side.
4. Then move a little bit of hair from the outside of the right side and cross it over and add it to the left side.
5. Keep going until you reach the end. Secure with an elastic.

It's really easy, and it looks really pretty!

Every so often, tighten the braid by pulling on the two sides of hair at the same time.

It's probably easiest if you lay your doll on the floor on her back and spread out her ponytail in front of you.

Learn more about Chloe on page 208!

Today Evan and I have to groom our dog, **Chloe**. Our mom helps.

My mom showers Chloe down when she gets muddy and stinky. Then I brush Chloe's hair and brush her teeth. **That's right—dogs need their hair and teeth brushed too!**

The hairbrush we use for Chloe is a smoothing brush with wire bristles. It's sharp but it doesn't hurt her. She really likes it. It makes her fluffy hair feel like a blanket. It's supersoft!

Now it's time to brush her teeth. Her toothpaste is peanut butter flavored. I kind of open her mouth with my hands so I can see her teeth. Then I brush them quickly.

We let her **rinse her mouth** by drinking water from a bowl. I dry her mouth with a towel, and then we give her a treat.

Dogs need their teeth brushed about once a week. But sometimes we forget, so Chloe's teeth get brushed every other week.

At the dinner table, my mom asks me **where I'd like to go for our next vacation**. Traveling is so much fun!

I've always wanted to go to **Italy**. I'm one quarter Italian, so that would be fun for a family trip. If I couldn't go there, I would choose **Paris**, France. I love going on family trips. Two of my favorite trips have been to New York City and Hong Kong.

New York City

Whenever we go to New York, we always go to the M&M'S World store in Times Square and pick out a bunch of candy. Even if we are tired because we took an overnight flight, we make sure we stop there. Evan and I tried caramel, minis, white chocolate, and more. As if that wasn't enough candy, we went down the street to Hershey's Chocolate World and saw the world's largest Hershey's bar. You can buy it! And giant Kit Kats and more.

The last time we were in New York, we saw a Broadway show, *SpongeBob SquarePants: The Broadway Musical*. The show was cool because

SpongeBob was a man—not a guy wearing a sponge costume. There was a lot of singing and dancing! I thought it was pretty good. Maybe someday I'll perform on Broadway.

Hong Kong

Hong Kong was so much fun. One of my favorite parts was when we went to **Ocean Park**, which is an animal theme park that also has a lot of rides. To get there, we had to take a ferry across Victoria Harbour. The first things we checked out were the giant pandas and some really cute monkeys.

Then we watched the penguins get fed. They were hungry! Then *we* were hungry. We went to a restaurant right next to where the penguins were swimming. It was so fun. We got to eat a cake that looked like a panda for dessert.

We also went to a carnival in the middle of the city, where we played a bunch of games and went on some rides like a giant slide and a giant swing. Then we went to a shopping district and got to shop for toys on "**Toy Street**." It was so cool! I loved the Hello Kitty Chinese Cuisine restaurant we went to right after. All the food was shaped like Hello Kitty. I never knew you could get Hello Kitty food!

The day can't end without doing **CRAFTS!** I like to sew by hand. To me, it is fun and relaxing. (Just not when I poke myself with the needle!) It's also fun to make little clothes and pillows for my family or my dolls.

I've done a lot of crafts on my channel, like:

- painting
- using a pottery wheel
- making DIY Play-Doh
- making DIY stress balls
- making a cardboard robot
- making gold slime, fluffy slime, scented slime, sparkly slime . . . and more!

DIY CARDBOARD ROBOT

I love cardboard, and I love making up crafts. Here's a craft I made up on my own: It's a robot! I named him Chris. Give it a try!

You will need:

tissue box	cardboard
gift wrap	paper plate
empty gift-wrap tube	3 straws
scissors	hot glue gun
tape	marker

1. Wrap a tissue box in gift wrap.

2. Cut the gift-wrap tube into four equal pieces for the arms and legs.

3. Cut four slits at one end of each cut tube to create tabs, then fold the tabs backward.

4. Tape the folded tabs of the arms and legs to the sides and bottom of the box.

5. Cut two feet shapes and two hand shapes out of cardboard. Ask an adult to use a hot glue gun to attach the feet to the legs and the hands to the arms. Let dry.

6. To make a face, draw eyes on a paper plate with a marker, cut them out, and glue them to the box. Use a straw for a mouth.

7. Now add two straws for antennae. Cut a slit in the end of each straw to create a tab, then fold the tabs backward. Attach to the head with tape.

⚠ DON'T TRY THIS YOURSELF. ALWAYS DO THIS WITH AN ADULT, ESPECIALLY WHEN USING SCISSORS OR THE HOT GLUE GUN.

147

8:00 p.m. *Bedtime . . . or Is It?*

Now it's time for bed, but I'm not tired yet. Hey! Do you want to stay up late and play games, like we're having a **sleepover**?

Let's play **Cool or Drool**. Here are the things I think are cool or boring (drool!). What about you?

HERE ARE MY ANSWERS!

Rainbows .... cool ★

Video games .... drool

Hedgehogs .... drool

Unicorns .... cool

Balloons .... cool

Snow .... cool

The beach .... cool

Candy corn .... drool knock-knock jokes .... cool

Pirates .... cool

Scary stories .... drool

Slime .... cool

Boogers .... drool

Stickers .... cool

Sleepovers .... cool

Pizza .... drool

Bugs .... drool

Dinosaurs .... drool

Baths .... cool

Now let's draw!

Check out these pictures I drew! Do you like drawing? What kinds of things do you like to draw?

Did you know? I'm left-handed!

YAY!

A PICTURE OF ME!

Whoops! Mom says we have to turn the lights out now. But that doesn't mean we have to stop chatting!

- If I had a superpower, I would like to shape-shift. It would be fun to be able to turn into different things.

- If I could invite one person onto my channel, I would invite **Hugh Jackman**, because he can sing and act. And I like the movie *The Greatest Showman*.

- When I go on YouTube, I watch **Easter egg videos**. "Easter eggs" are hidden items, like hidden Mickeys in a Disney movie. I like to see if I can find the Easter eggs in my favorite movies.

The one thing I can't live without is . . . my family!

They help guide me along and teach me new things.

When I'm fifteen years old . . . I hope I'm doing **YouTube videos** and maybe making a lot more craft videos.

When I'm twenty-five years old . . . I hope I'll be on **a farm** riding horses, milking the cows, and playing with the pigs in the mud. Like my mom says, I don't mind getting dirty!

Find out Jillian's dream job and more on page 203!

8:30 p.m. *Good Night!*

I'm finally getting sleepy. . . . Good night!

Thanks for hanging out, and see you on my channel!

How well do you know Jillian? Take the ULTIMATE JillianTubeHD and EvanTubeHD Quiz on page 220.

157

Sweet Dreams!

I dream about . . .

Unicorns!

Glitter!

A bunch
of slime!

Monkeys!

Rainbows!

Meet Evan from EvanTube HD™

Hi! I'm Evan!

Age: 12
Height: 59 inches
(almost 5 feet!)
Hair color: brown
Eye color: brown

I'm Evan from EvanTubeHD! I'm Jillian's older brother! I've been making YouTube videos with my family since 2011. My videos are all about toys, challenges, video games, science experiments, and more. If I had to pick one word to describe myself, it would be **"creative"**!

My Favorite . . .

Ice cream flavor: rainbow sherbet

Food: pizza (obviously the best food in the universe)

Subject: I guess math is pretty cool.

Animal: otter or monkey (They both are so cute!)

Holiday: Christmas

Season: winter

TV show: *Stranger Things* or *Steven Universe*

(They are both great shows with great stories.)

Color: red

Drink: Dr Pepper

Number: 64

Emoji: 😎

Superhero: The Flash

Watch Me!

Ate: **3**

Wore: **13**

Evan
1

Jillian
1

How I Got Started

When I was five years old, I thought it would be cool to try to make my own YouTube video. My dad and I made a stop-motion video featuring Angry Birds plush toys and uploaded it on the very same day. It was only thirty seconds long. It was very simple but I was so proud of it. We thought our friends and family would be the only ones who saw it.

How Things Have Changed

We used to do a lot of videos with clay models and plushies. It's cool how those videos are so different from the videos I post today. Now we make videos about toys, we do challenges, and we make arts-and-crafts videos—and tons more people watch them! We're going to start doing animation, which will be really cool.

Try It at Home: Stop Motion

Stop motion is when you stitch together a series of photos to make something look like it's moving. With each photo, you move the object a tiny bit. When you click through the photos quickly, it looks like a movie. Stop-motion software can help make this process a lot easier.

Inside EvanTubeHD

SUBSCRIBERS: 5.6 million+
UPLOADING SINCE: September 2011
TOTAL VIEWS: 3.4 billion+
OTHER CHANNELS: EvanTubeRAW, EvanTubeGaming

Q: What are your favorite toys?

A: My favorite toys are LEGOs. I love them a lot because of the creativity. I also like collectibles because I like to put them on a shelf in my bedroom.

My Longest Video to Film

It took me more than a week to build and review the LEGO Death Star from Star Wars. It has almost four thousand pieces and was meant for kids age fourteen and up. I was only seven years old! It was one of the biggest sets I'd ever built.

After school, I'd do my homework and then build a little bit more each day. My dad helped with some parts, like attaching the stickers because I couldn't put them on straight. We made a time-lapse video that shows me building the whole thing in three minutes.

Try It at Home: Time-Lapse Video

Time-lapse videos are like the opposite of slow motion. They show a long period of time sped up really fast. The easiest way to make one is with a phone or tablet that has a time-lapse setting. Make sure to keep the camera in the same position during the recording.

My Most-Watched Video

It's me eating a giant gummy worm—the world's largest gummy worm! It weighed three pounds and was twenty-six inches long. It tasted good. In the skit, I share the gummy worm with my sister and a friend. The video has been viewed more than 132 million times. Can you believe it?!

Q: What's your favorite part of being on YouTube?

A: Honestly, I think it's making people smile. Be happy. All that jazz.

Q: What's your least favorite part of being on YouTube?

A: Trolls and haters. I know to just ignore it. But they can be annoying.

My Favorite Video

It's hard to pick a favorite, but I really enjoy going back and watching my older videos where I was much younger. They make me laugh! Recently, I liked watching the "Simon Swipe Showdown" skit, the "Fixits" video, and my second video where I review my Angry Birds clay models.

Q: What inspires you?

A: Some of my favorite YouTubers who influence my video style. For example, there is a web series called Game Theory whose comedic style I really enjoy.

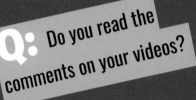

"Simon Swipe Showdown"

We got to create a cool skit about a new game called Simon Swipe. In the skit, we find a time machine and then get to meet "Future Evan" and "Future Jillian." I look the same except I have a mustache! We challenge each other to play the game. You'll have to watch the video to see who wins.

The "Fixits" Video

This was a TV pilot we shot with Disney XD by Maker. Not only did Jillian and I get to act in it, but our parents did too. We got to fight an evil robot and save our parents from getting destroyed. It was awesome!

A TV pilot is a sample episode for a television series.

Review of Angry Birds Clay Figures

We made this video in 2011. I was so little! I just hold up some Angry Birds clay figures that my dad and I made, and I talk about their colors and their powers. There are even some characters that we made up, like a mustache panda bear. Ha!

Q: Do you read the comments on your videos?

A: Yes. After we upload a video, we wait about an hour or so, and then we sit and read some comments, laugh at them, and sometimes respond to them.

My Sister, Jillian!

I have a younger sister named Jillian. You probably know her because she appears in a lot of my videos. She even has her own YouTube channel, JillianTubeHD. She's funny and crazy, which makes my videos a lot more fun to make.

Q: What's it like filming videos as siblings?

A: Evan: I'm nicer to my sister on camera than in real life. 😄 But hey, if I'm mean, JILL STARTED IT!!! But yeah, I'm pretty nice, as far as older brothers go.

A: Jillian: Usually we get along, but sometimes we get on each other's nerves.

Q: What's one word you'd use to describe your sibling?

A: Evan: Crazy!

A: Jillian: Hey, that's what I was going to say!

Learn even more about Jillian in her section, which starts on page 109!

The Sibling Challenge: Evan vs. Jillian

My favorite kinds of videos are the challenges, and I bet Jillian's favorite videos are anytime where she beats me at a challenge.

We're going to play the Sibling Challenge today! First Jillian will guess my favorite things. Then I'll guess Jillian's favorite things. Whoever gets more guesses correct wins. The person who loses has to make their silliest faces at the camera!

Jillian guesses my favorite . . .

Ice cream flavor: Oreo ✗

Food: pizza
(Of course you got this one! —Evan)

Subject: math

Movie: *Back to the Future*

Animal: dogs ✗

Book: Harry Potter series
(More specifically, *Harry Potter and the Goblet of Fire.* —Evan)

Holiday: Christmas

Season: winter

TV show: *Stranger Things*

Color: red, blue, and purple ✗
(Nice guesses, but it's just red. —Evan)

Drink: Sprite ✗

Number: 64

Emoji: 💩 ✗
(Wrong, it's 🤩. —Evan)

FINAL SCORE
8

Ice cream flavor: peppermint

Food: calamari ✘

Subject: math

Animal: unicorn ✘
(You're close! —Jillian)

Book: the Magic Tree House series ✘

Place to visit: Los Angeles, CA ✘

Holiday: Christmas

Season: summer

Color: pink ✘
(Almost! It's magenta! —Jillian)

Drink: root beer ✘

Number: 8

Hobby: annoying her brother ✘
(Nice try, but it's singing! —Jillian)

Emoji: ✘
(Nope, it's . —Jillian)

FINAL SCORE
5

I thought Jillian's favorite food was calamari, which is fried squid. I was wrong—it's mashed potatoes! Turn to page 111 to learn more about Jillian's favorites.

And the winner is . . .

JILLIAN!

Since I lost the sibling challenge, I have to make a bunch of **funny faces**. Well, here goes nothing!

A Day in My Life

Mon	Tue	Wed	Thu	Fri	Sat	Sun

Good morning!

I get up early. On my bed I have a bunch of plushies. There are even more plushies on the floor. It's like an ocean of plushies (and dirty laundry) that I like to swim through.

Then I get dressed and have breakfast. Belgian waffles are my favorite! What do you like to eat for breakfast?

179

After breakfast, I get in the car and go to school. My parents drive us to school every day. My sister and I go to different schools.

At school, a lot of people are fans, and they say, **"Hey, what's up?"**

What It's Like to Be Recognized

It feels good when people recognize me, because it means that they like what I'm doing. Sometimes it feels strange because I don't see myself as a famous person!

Jillian and I have done "meet and greets" before, where we get to meet our fans in person. One time we had more than one thousand people come to Downtown Disney to meet us. We stayed an extra hour so we could meet them all!

Q: What do you think about the millions of people watching you?

A: They are awesome. If they like the content I create, great! They all are really supportive, and I love that about them.

Some of the fans screamed when they saw us. It was crazy. We took a lot of pictures and selfies, gave hugs and high fives, and signed autographs. Some fans even made art for us, which was really nice. By the end of the day, it was hard to smile because we had smiled so much!

What I'd Like Fans to Know

If you're a fan who's meeting someone you admire for the first time, maybe take it slow. Don't just scream, but make your way up to the person, say hi, and then give them a chance to become comfortable.

Q: What's the one question that fans always ask you?

A: "Can I get a picture with you?"

Q: What's the craziest thing that's happened with a fan?

A: There was this one time that a little boy followed me into a movie theater bathroom. THAT was crazy.

A lot of fans at school ask me **questions** about my channel. They also ask me for advice on becoming a **YouTuber**, so I try my best to answer them.

Q: Do you keep the toys or products you review on your channel?

A: I can keep them if I want. But I don't need so many toys, so we donate some of them to charity.

Q: Which room in the house would you not want a camera?

A: The bathroom.

Jillian
4

Q: Is there a time of the day when you never film?

A: When I'm out with my friends, I don't film it.

Q: How do you decide what kind of videos to make?

A: Just do what you're passionate about. If you want to make a video, just do what you want to do, and be creative about it.

Q: How do you come up with creative ideas for videos?

A: Either random ideas popping into my head, viewer suggestions, or subjects that are popular.

MOST VIEWED VIDEO
UNBOXING VIDEO
A YouTube video of the *Minecraft* Papercraft Overworld Deluxe Set being unpackaged and assembled by "EvanTubeHD" had attracted 19,476,399 views by 23 Aug 2016.

Did you know?
I was in *Guinness World Records* in 2017! I set the record for "Most viewed videogame unboxing video." The video was about the *Minecraft* Papercraft Overworld Deluxe Set. It's been watched over 26 million times! We got a framed certificate to hang on our wall.

My school day is probably a lot like yours: language arts, math, reading, phys ed, social studies, and of course—lunch!

At school, sometimes I buy lunch and sometimes I bring a lunch. I like **pizza**, breadsticks, yogurt parfaits, and fries.

I like pizza, pizza, and a side of pizza.

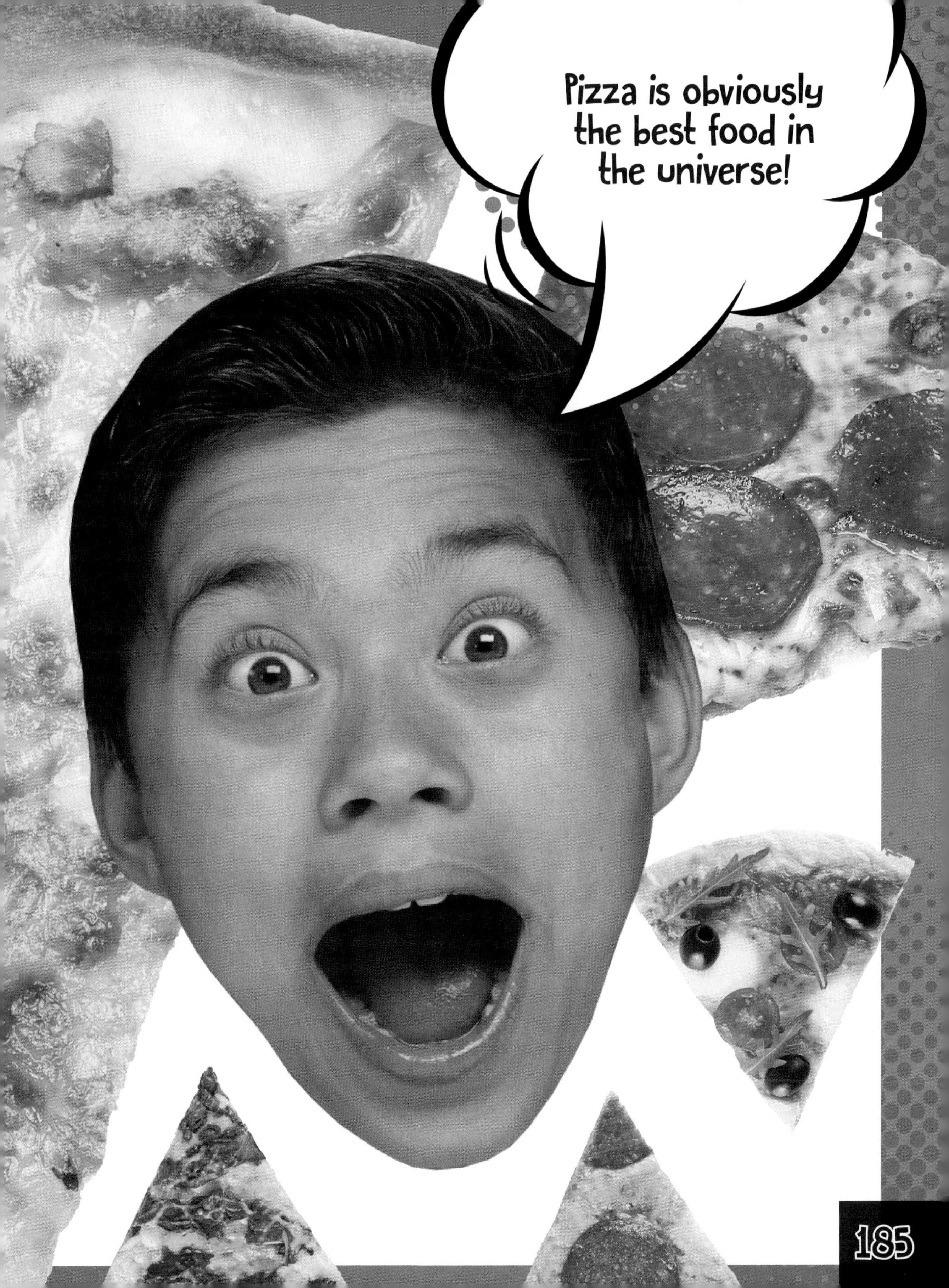
Pizza is obviously the best food in the universe!

Did I mention I like pizza?

If I could spend a day doing whatever I wanted, I would . . .

☺ Eat pizza. And draw and make animation.

☺ Do whatever I want.

☺ Go on the computer for twenty-four hours straight.

☺ Go bike riding.

☺ Play video games for as long as I wanted to.

☺ Eat candy.

☺ Eat more pizza!

Back to reality. In class today, we talk about what we want to do when we grow up.

If I could peek into a crystal ball and see my future, I would see . . .

When I'm seventeen years old . . .

I'll probably still be doing **YouTube**, but changing up the format—doing different kinds of videos. After all, I've been making videos for most of my life now!

When I'm twenty-seven years old . . .

I hope I'm an **animator**, because that's something I want to pursue. I'd like to work for any cartoon company, like Pixar, or make my own animations. I want to make some kind of cartoon that will stand out.

3:30 p.m. *After School*

My afternoons are busy! I go from:

school

to track and field

then come home

then do homework.

Besides homework, I have some **chores** to do too. I'm on **garbage** duty, but I also clean the **bathroom**, wash the **dishes**, and feed my **dog**.

I don't get an allowance, but if I do chores, I can earn more screen time. Otherwise I only get one hour of screen time per day.

I can't live without . . .
WI-FI AND MY COMPUTER.
When I go on YouTube, I watch comedy videos, video game videos, music videos, animation, and pranks.

GAME OVER

Q: If you could invite a famous person on your channel, who would it be?

A: MatPat from the web series Game Theory.

Sometimes I do a video after school. My dad and I started a gaming channel called **EvanTubeGaming** just so we could play video games and share experiences together.

His reactions are pretty hilarious. It's fun! I think people like watching us play, especially when there's an iconic moment in a video game. People like to see our reactions.

Try It at Home: Gaming Videos

Have you ever wanted to film yourself playing a video game? PlayStation 4 and Xbox One have settings that let you record video game footage, edit it, and share it. You can even save your audio from a microphone.

My top three favorite video games are **Fortnite**, *Undertale*, and **Super Mario Odyssey**. You can watch me play these games on EvanTubeGaming.

Fortnite is a co-op game where you have to fight off zombies in order to survive. I'm not the best at it, but I won one game. It's hard! The Battle Royale is a one-hundred-player PvP (player versus player). PvP means you're playing against other gamers like you instead of a computer player. You don't get to pick your character. It's random every time.

Undertale is a role-playing game where you are a kid who is trying to escape the Underground and return to Earth's surface by fighting off monsters. If you're younger, you might want to stay away, because there are some scary parts.

Super Mario Odyssey is a really fun Nintendo Switch game. Mario and Cappy have to beat various worlds to save Princess Peach from Bowser. I've posted a bunch of videos on my gaming channel about this one!

Q: Do you have any advice for gamers who want to get better?

A: Keep practicing. The more you play, the better you get. You can also watch videos of me and my dad playing games. That way you can see how we play it. It's like a learning experience, in a way.

I couldn't make my videos without my parents!

Before we started making YouTube videos together, my dad ran his own video production company, and my mom was a teacher. They both have an acting background and met while performing in a show.

Q: Do you have any advice for making great videos?

A: DaddyTube: Have fun with it! If you don't, it will show up in your work.

DaddyTube

When we started EvanTubeHD, we thought that only our family and friends would be watching. But soon we were posting all kinds of videos, and a lot of people were watching! We have four minds to draw ideas from for our videos.

Q: What do you want to be doing ten years from now?

A: DaddyTube: Visiting the kids in college.

Q: What do you like to watch on YouTube?

A: DaddyTube: Music videos and tech reviews.

DaddyTube has his own YouTube channel called DTSings.

Q: What did you do before making YouTube videos?

A: MommyTube: I taught kindergarten.

MommyTube

I love making vlogs with the family. It's an activity we do together and we watch them over and over again. We always get a kick out of watching old videos.

Try It at Home: Vlog

"Vlog" is short for "video blog." It's like a diary, but instead of writing things down, you're recording video. Try making some of your own!

Q: What do you like to watch on YouTube?

A: MommyTube: DIY (do-it-yourself) videos.

Q: Do you have any advice for making great videos?

Find our family vlogs on our EvanTubeRAW channel.

A: MommyTube: Try to keep things positive and light. Humor goes over really well.

195

More from MommyTube and DaddyTube!

Want to start a channel with your family? MommyTube and DaddyTube have some tips for making great memories.

🔊 Make your videos as interesting as possible. After each toy review, we do something with the toy that it wasn't meant to do. Creativity is the big thing on YouTube. The more creative you can get, the more entertaining it will be.

🔊 Be a good role model. That's a huge message we want to put across: be a positive influence. We try to stay away from anything that may be considered inappropriate. We know we have a lot of young people watching.

🔊 Consider what you're putting out there. The world is watching, and these videos don't go away once they're published. Look over things and re-look over things before you push that publish button.

🔊 Keep personal things out of your videos. If you're trying to protect your privacy, make sure no street signs, landmarks, or school shirts end up on camera. You have to be diligent.

🔊 Have fun. If you're having a good time, chances are your audience is going to have a good time watching.

Q: Did you ever film an episode, then realize, "This didn't work"?

A: We've had that happen a few times with vlogs that didn't turn out as exciting as we had imagined. When it happens it's not a big deal, we just move on to the next thing.

Q: What's been your favorite part of being on YouTube?

A: Our favorite part has definitely been the awesome things the kids have gotten to experience, like traveling to different places and meeting and working with amazing people.

Q: What's been your least favorite part of being on YouTube?

A: Dealing with haters and critics. There's always going to be people who are negative.

Q: How do you deal with online bullies?

A: We know not to take it personally. They say things not necessarily because they are true but because maybe they don't feel good about themselves or they want to hurt others.

Q: Do you need fancy equipment to shoot a good YouTube video?

A: No. The audience will appreciate it as long as it has a good story and is entertaining.

When I'm not filming, I'm usually composing digital music. I am pretty good at composing music, which I haven't posted to my channel—YET. I like to listen to video game remixes and even compose my own. The ones I enjoy the most are ones from the game *Undertale*.

Try It at Home: Compose Digital Music

I use a software called FL Studio to create music. I learned to make music by messing around until it sounds right. First, I create a melody, then add drums, and finally add bass. After that, I make the track and add other effects.

What does "composing" music mean? It means creating a whole piece of music. You have to make decisions like what notes and what instruments to use.

I also like coding games with GameMaker, watching TV, and reading. My favorite kind of books are sci-fi, horror, and mystery. But my all-time favorite book is *Harry Potter and the Goblet of Fire.*

WHAT?!

WOW!!

COOL!!

I DREW THESE!

You might not know this, but I love drawing. I also create digital art! Here is some of my **recent artwork**.

It's late afternoon now, and Jillian tells me that she played **Would You Rather** with her friends at lunchtime today. That game is so much fun! Jillian asks me the questions she played at school. My answers are highlighted in green below. What would you pick?

Would you rather . . .

Turn to page 126 to read Jillian's Would You Rather answers!

tell the truth ↖or↗ do a dare?

swim in a pool ↖or↗ swim in the ocean?

live on the moon ↖or↗ **live under the sea**?

be able to read minds ↖or↗ have X-ray vision?

go back in time ↖or↗ **go into the future**?

stand forever ↖or↗ **sit forever**?

eat ice cream for every meal ↖or↗ eat candy for every meal?

eat all your vegetables every day ↖or↗ **take a bath every day**?

stay up late ↖or↗ get up early?

have hair that sticks up all the time ↖or↗ have no hair at all?

201

6:00 p.m. *Dinnertime!*

Now it's time for dinner. My favorite dinner is pizza, obviously, but I also like chicken nuggets and mac and cheese. Jillian's favorite dinner is spaghetti, breadsticks, tacos, or Dad's chicken stir-fry.

Q: What do you want to be when you grow up?

 A: I want to be an animator.

 A: I want to be a singer and dancer. Or maybe act in films.

Q: What makes you laugh?

A: Funny dog videos, horrible puns, and my dog.

A: If someone makes a funny face or tickles me, it makes me laugh really hard.

Q: If you were stranded on a deserted island, what would you bring?

A: Pizza, video games, and a computer. Oh, and I SUPPOSE healthy food to keep me alive. Oh, wait, I need water too. . . .

 A: I would bring water and food for sure. Also, some shelter.

Over dinner we also talk about all the cool places we've been to recently. Some of the best parts about being on YouTube is that I get to travel to cool places, meet new people, and try new things.

If I could go anywhere in the world, I'd go to **Hawaii.** We've been there a few times. It's really fun. I like swimming in the pool, the nice beaches, and the water slides. My whole family went down a really steep water slide at the Disney Aulani resort. My mom screamed so loud that it sounded like she was singing opera. Everyone could hear her—ha!

I also like shaved ice a lot. It's like a snow cone, but the ice is shaved instead of crushed. It's very popular in Hawaii. You can also add a scoop of vanilla ice cream to it. I love the cherry flavor because that's my favorite fruit.

Also, pineapple and grape. You usually pick three flavors when you order shaved ice. At the Aulani resort, the shaved ice has Mickey ears. It's so good!

Where Else
Have We Gone?

I also got to go to the Nintendo of America headquarters near Seattle, Washington, and it was such a fun experience. I was only there for one day, but I'm convinced I want to move to Seattle.

The Nintendo headquarters was cool. I got to do a tour for an event with a bunch of other kids. We decorated Nintendo-themed holiday cookies and got to meet the president of Nintendo of America as well as some of the characters. I wore a mustache and got a pic with Mario and Luigi!

But the best part of the day was when we got to demo some of the new games that were coming out in time for Christmas. I played *Super Mario Maker*, *Yo-kai Watch*, *Super Smash Bros.*, and more. Seriously, it was a whole day of gaming! It was impossible to pick a favorite game.

Every night I make sure **Chloe** gets dinner too. Our dog, Chloe, is a goldendoodle. She's just three years old, but she's already really big. If she stands up on her hind legs, she's taller than Jillian!

I named her Chloe after a character I liked on a TV show. But sometimes we call her **PuppyTube**.

Jillian and I feed the dog, but our parents have to walk her. Chloe's hard to walk because she's so heavy. She pulls us!

Chloe is very energetic. She likes to play with toys, chase us, and take our shoes. We call her Crazy Chloe!

We got Chloe for Christmas one year. She was a gift from our parents and a total surprise! Jillian and I already had other pets, like a newt, a tortoise, a snake, and a gecko, but we really wanted a dog. Dad said we were never getting one, so I thought I'd have to wait until I was eighteen and get one on my own.

Jillian and I had no idea, but then we saw one last box on Christmas morning. The box was kind of moving and kind of crying. We knew it had to be a dog. I took the lid off the box, and what do you know, it was a puppy! Jillian jumped up and down and screamed.

We couldn't believe we got a puppy—and that everyone had kept her a secret from us.

Goldendoodles are a cross between a golden retriever and a poodle. They're so cute!

Chloe's so excited for her food. She's wagging her tail and barking and drooling everywhere.

Hey, do you want to play a game of **Cool or Drool**? My answers are below. What about you? What do you think is cool? What do you think is boring (drool)?

HERE ARE MY ANSWERS!

Rainbows ·························· cool

Video games ·························· cool

Hedgehogs ·························· cool

Unicorns ·························· cool

Balloons ·························· cool

Snow ·························· cool

The beach ·························· cool

Candy corn ·························· drool

Knock-knock jokes .... cool

Pirates .... cool

Scary stories .... cool

Slime .... cool

Boogers .... drool

Stickers .... drool

Sleepovers .... cool

Pizza .... cool

Bugs .... drool

Dinosaurs .... cool

Baths .... cool

9:00 p.m. *Good Night!*

Okay, time for bed. I hope I dream about teleporting, maybe like Marty McFly does in *Back to the Future* (that's my favorite movie, a classic).

I would really like to teleport. Like, REALLY bad.

I also like the movie *Coco*, which has a very intriguing plot.

In our Simon Swipe video, "Future Evan" and "Future Jillian" traveled back in time to meet us. Wouldn't that be crazy to meet your future self? Do you think you'd like what you'd see?

Well, that was a typical EvanTubeHD day.
Good night, and thanks for reading about me!
See you again on my channel!

How well do you know Evan? Take the ULTIMATE JillianTubeHD and EvanTubeHD Quiz on page 220.

Ultimate Quizzes!

The ULTIMATE Ryan ToysReview Quiz!

How well do you know Ryan? Take this quiz to find out!

1. How would Ryan describe himself?
   a. quiet
   b. shy
   c. curious

2. What is Ryan's favorite drink?
   a. milk
   b. orange juice
   c. water

3. How old was Ryan when he made his first YouTube video?
   a. three years old
   b. six years old
   c. ten years old

4. What are Ryan's sisters' names?
   a. Evan and Jillian
   b. Emma and Kate
   c. Jillian and Kate

5. What was Ryan's mom's job before making YouTube videos?
   a. chemistry teacher
   b. actress
   c. professional swimmer

6. What is Ryan's favorite school subject?
   a. math
   b. gym
   c. none—Ryan doesn't go to school!

7. Ryan's dad surprised Ryan with a trip to which country?
   a. Australia
   b. France
   c. Japan

8. How many cats does Ryan have?

    a. two hundred!

    b. twenty

    c. two

9. What does Ryan want to be when he grows up?

    a. singer

    b. game developer

    c. astronaut

10. BONUS CHALLENGE QUESTION: Which toy has Ryan actually reviewed on his channel?

    a. Lightning McQueen Power Wheels ride-on car

    b. invisible glittery slime

    c. inflatable underwater trampoline

Turn to page 224 to check your answers!

If you got 0–2 questions correct . . . try again!
Are you sure you watched this book?

If you got 3–5 questions correct . . . you're a subscriber!
Good job, but you can do even better! Keep watching!

If you got 6–9 questions correct . . . you're a mega-fan!
Wow, your knowledge of Ryan ToysReview is impressive!

If you got 10 questions correct . . . ARE YOU RYAN??
You got all the questions right! How did you do that?

Are you possibly . . .
RYAN HIMSELF??

WOW!

The ULTIMATE HobbykidsTV Quiz!

How well do you know the HobbyKids? Take this quiz to find out!

1. Who is the oldest Hobbykid?
   a. HobbyBear
   b. HobbyPig
   c. HobbyFrog

2. Who is the middle Hobbykid?
   a. HobbyBear
   b. HobbyPig
   c. HobbyFrog

3. Who is the youngest Hobbykid?
   a. HobbyBear
   b. HobbyPig
   c. HobbyFrog

4. What are the Hobbykids most famous for?
   a. their surprise eggs
   b. their disco dance moves
   c. their weekly epic fail videos

5. What would all the Hobbykids do on their best day ever?
   a. visit the moon
   b. watch SpongeBob SquarePants
   c. go to sleep at midnight

6. What color is their pet dog, Flappy?
   a. yellow
   b. white
   c. red

7. When do the Hobbykids come up with video ideas?
   a. while they're sleeping
   b. while they're at school
   c. anytime!

8. If HobbyFrog could visit any place in the world, where would he go?
   a. Legoland
   b. the North Pole
   c. nowhere—he likes to stay home

9. What does HobbyBear mean when he says "slippery bacon"?
   a. bacon with no crispy parts
   b. bacon made out of Play-Doh
   c. it's the name of his favorite toy

10. Why does HobbyPig like rainbows?
    a. because unicorns fart them
    b. because they're sparkly and colorful
    c. trick question—he doesn't like rainbows

Turn to page 224 to check your answers!

If you got 0–2 questions correct . . . you're a HobbyStranger.
Are you sure you watched this book?

If you got 3–5 questions correct . . . you're a HobbySubscriber!
Good job, but you can do even better! Keep watching!

If you got 6–9 questions correct . . . you're a HobbyFriend!
Wow, you know a lot about the HobbyKids!

If you got 10 questions correct . . . welcome to the HobbyFamily!

You know them so well, you're basically part of the HobbyKids family!

The ULTIMATE JillianTubeHD and EvanTubeHD Quiz!

How well do you know Evan and Jillian? Take this quiz to find out!

1. Who does Evan play with on his EvanTubeGaming channel?
   a. Chloe
   b. DanTDM
   c. DaddyTube

2. What is Evan's most-watched video?
   a. giant gummy worm skit
   b. Angry Birds plushie review
   c. DIY slime video

3. What song did Jillian sing at a football game?
   a. "Happy Birthday"
   b. "Take Me Out to the Ball Game"
   c. the national anthem

4. What does Evan want to be when he grows up?
   a. animator
   b. singer
   c. teacher

5. What is Evan's favorite food?
   a. pizza
   b. pizza
   c. pizza
   d. all of the above!

6. What is Jillian's favorite animal?
   a. horses
   b. alligators
   c. pigeons

7. What pet do Evan and Jillian own?
   a. parrot
   b. dog
   c. goldfish

8. Which activity does Jillian *not* do after school?
   a. Zumba
   b. choir
   c. volleyball

9. If Jillian could go anywhere in the world, where would she go?
   a. Italy
   b. Japan
   c. Mexico

10. When do Evan and Jillian usually film their videos?

    a. in the morning

    b. on the weekends

    c. at three a.m.!

Turn to page 224 to check your answers!

If you got 0–2 questions correct . . . try again!

Are you sure you watched this book?

If you got 3–5 questions correct . . . you're a subscriber!

Good job, but you can do even better! Keep watching!

If you got 6–9 questions correct . . . you're a mega-fan!

Wow, your knowledge of EvanTubeHD and JillianTubeHD is impressive!

If you got 10 questions correct . . . congratulations!

You're amazing! Treat yourself to some **pizza!**

What Do You Do with
ALL THOSE TOYS?!

As YouTube toy reviewers, we get a lot of toys. That's no secret! We have a ton of fun testing out the toys and games for the camera, but the truth is, we don't need them all. **We donate most of what you see on our channels!**

Have you ever donated something to charity? When you donate to a charity, it means that instead of just sitting in your room gathering dust, that toy or game gets to be loved by another kid. That's pretty awesome, right?

Here are some tips that will help you decide which toys to donate:

1. Ask yourself: have you played with the toy or game in the past year? If not, you probably won't miss it. Think of all the other kids out there who could put this toy or game to use.

2. Follow this rule: one toy in, one toy out. Before you use your allowance to buy a new toy, you donate an old one. It will make you realize how much you already have.

3. Organize your toys. Every toy should have a special place, whether it's a bin, a shelf, or a basket. When you're organized, it's easier to play with your favorites. And while you organize, you might realize there are a few toys you don't need anymore.

Here are some charities that are always looking for toys:

Goodwill
The Salvation Army
Ronald McDonald House
Toys for Tots
Local homeless shelters
Local Boys & Girls Clubs
Local preschools, day cares, or nurseries

These organizations take kids' books too (so do many libraries)!

Make sure the toys, games, and books aren't broken. They should be clean and in good condition.

Thanks for watching this book!
Come visit us on our YouTube channels!

Ryan ToysReview: www.youtube.com/ryantoysreview

HobbyKidsTV: www.youtube.com/hobbykidstv

JillianTubeHD: www.youtube.com/jilliantubehd

EvanTubeHD: www.youtube.com/evantubehd

CaptainSparklez: www.youtube.com/captainsparklez

QUIZ ANSWERS

Ryan ToysReview

1. c   2. a   3. a   4. b   5. a   6. a   7. c   8. c   9. b   10. a

HobbykidsTV

1. b   2. c   3. a   4. a   5. b   6. c   7. c   8. a   9. a   10. a

JillianTubeHD and EvanTubeHD

1. c   2. a   3. c   4. a   5. d   6. a   7. b   8. c   9. a   10. b